Advance praise for this book

"A how-to classic."
—*The Washington Post*

"An invaluable tool, infinitely wise, and very practical. No businessperson should be without this handy guide."
—Kenneth S. Olshan,
Chairman of the Board and CEO,
Wells Rich Greene BDDP, Inc.

"The basis of all motivation is communication. To be a successful communicator requires discipline, understanding, and verve. Joan Detz understands this, and provides a firm foundation from which to launch influential communications."
—James S. Todd, M.D.
Executive Vice President, the American
Medical Association

"This book is a practical text for helping anyone develop the ability to learn to speak and to become more visible and effective."
—Terrence J. McCann
Executive Director, Toastmasters
International

"In international business, knowing how to speak efficiently and effectively is the key to success. This handy book will help busy executives master this important skill."
—Dr. Mitsuru Misawa, President,
International Bank of Japan Leasing (USA) Inc., and
Director, IBJ Leasing (Tokyo)

Praise for *Can You Say a Few Words?*

"Let me say a few words about Joan Detz: Her books are great."
—Roger Ailes, top presidential and
corporate communications consultant,
and author of
You Are the Message

"*Can You Say a Few Words?* by Joan Detz has helped me to speak better. I recommend this book to anyone who wishes to use words well."
—Norman Vincent Peale, author of
The Power of Positive Thinking

"Joan Detz's book *Can You Say a Few Words?* is imaginative, practical, and necessary. All of us who are asked to speak can learn a great deal from it. Keep it close by."
—Stephen D. Harlan, Vice Chairman,
KPMG Peat Marwick

"Once again, Joan Detz has packed her new book with helpful tips for the novice as well as the experienced presenter . . . better yet, she does it with such good humor, *Can You Say a Few Words?* is actually an enjoyable and fast read."
—Hans Decker, Vice Chairman,
Siemens Corporation

"This book is filled with enough great advice and memorable quotes to spice up dozens of speeches. It's like having a personal speech writer and presentation coach available at a moment's notice. Even the most experienced speaker will find something new and valuable in this book."
—Alan M. Silberstein,
Executive Vice President,
Chemical Bank

"A very helpful, very practical book."
—Rabbi Harold S. Kushner, author of
When Bad Things Happen to Good People

How to Write and
Give a Speech

Other books by Joan Detz:

You Mean I Have to Stand Up & Say Something?
Can You Say a Few Words?

How to
Write and
Give a Speech

——————————— ✳ ✳ ———————————

A practical guide for executives,

PR people, managers, fund-raisers, politicians,

educators, and anyone who

has to make every word count

Joan Detz

St. Martin's Press·New York

Production Editor: David Stanford Burr

Design by Tanya M. Pérez

Library of Congress Cataloging-in-Publication Data

Detz, Joan.
     How to write and give a speech / Joan Detz. — Rev. ed.
         p.   cm.
     Includes index.
     ISBN 0-312-08504-4 — ISBN 0-312-08218-5 (pbk.)
     1. Public speaking.   I. Title.
PN4121.D388 1992
808.5′1—dc20   92-25478
                                                    CIP

Second Edition: October 1992

10 9 8 7 6 5 4 3 2 1

For my clients

As a speechwriter and speech coach,
I've had the pleasure of working with
many outstanding businesspeople—
executives with keen minds,
fresh perspectives, and articulate voices.
This book is dedicated to them all . . .
with my admiration, my appreciation,
and my very best wishes.

Acknowledgments

This new edition of *How to Write and Give a Speech* reflects the good efforts of many people. In particular, I would like to thank:

- My editor, Barbara Anderson. She believed in this book right from the start.

- The reference librarians at the Brooklyn Business Library. They always knew the answers.

- The librarians at the main branch of the Bucks County Free Library in Doylestown, Pennsylvania. They were unfailingly helpful in tracking down so many details.

- The booksellers who stocked the original edition back in 1984—when *How to Write and Give a Speech* was just another new title hoping to get some shelf space. These booksellers gave my book a chance to prove itself—and then steadily kept reordering copies over the years. What more could any author want?

- My husband, Ira Rubinstein. He generously helped with the editing and the proofreading, and offered valuable suggestions along the way.

- My son, Seth. He was born shortly after I completed this manuscript. With his birth, he gave me the greatest gift of all—a new perspective. And for this, he gets my most special "thank you."

Contents

Appendix: Useful Reference Books from the Author's Personal Library   179

Index   194

How to Write and
Give a Speech

Introduction

✳

The reason a lot of people do not recognize opportunity is
because it usually goes around wearing overalls looking
like hard work.
—Thomas Edison

Fair question:

Why come out with a new edition of *How to Write & Give
a Speech?* And, why *now?*

Because when this book was originally published back in
the early 1980s, the ability to give a good speech was an
important skill. Now, as we move through the 90s toward the
new century, the ability to give a good speech has become an
absolutely *critical* skill—a skill that can provide business people with a competitive edge.

You see, organizations aren't concerned only about what
their speeches might *say.* Increasingly, they're concerned
about what their speeches can *do.*

Big corporations, small businesses, nonprofit agencies,
educational institutions, cultural organizations, political leaders . . . they're *all* asking (or, maybe I should say, *demanding*),
"What can a good speech do for *us?*"

And, as a professional speechwriter, I'd like to say, "A
good speech can do a *lot.*" A good speech can:

- motivate employees

- rev up a sales team

- calm disgruntled shareholders
- spark interest in a new service
- launch a successful campaign
- build credibility
- clarify the real issues
- correct public misconceptions
- garner community support
- persuade voters
- create rapport with government leaders
- position an executive as a highly competent, caring, and dynamic leader
- present the organization as a responsible, concerned corporate citizen
- generate valuable publicity
- and . . . a good speech can pay for itself *many times over.*

In fact, I'd like to go on record as saying:

A good speech is the single most cost-effective marketing and public relations tool any organization can have. (And, yes, you can quote me on that.)

With this new, updated version—geared to meet today's business demands as we move toward the twenty-first century—I'd like to show you how to write and give a speech that will produce solid, substantial benefits for *your* organization.

Read on . . . make notes . . . and learn how to prepare a powerful speech that will give *you* the competitive edge.

My best wishes!

So You've Been Asked to Give a Speech. . . . Now What?

Half the world is composed of people who have
something to say and can't—and the other half who have
nothing to say and keep on saying it.
—Robert Frost

So, you've just been asked to give a speech.

Do you race to the library to do some research? Do you hunt for some introductory jokes? Do you pull together some statistics? Not if you're smart.

DETERMINE WHAT YOU WANT TO SAY

Begin, instead, by asking yourself, "What do I *really* want to say?" And then be ruthless in your answer. You have to focus your subject. You can't include everything in one speech.

Let me repeat that so it sinks in:

You can't include everything in one speech. In fact, if you try to include *everything,* your audience will probably come away with *nothing.* Decide what you really want to say, and don't throw in any other material.

For example, if you're speaking to a community group about your corporate ethics, don't think you have to give them a complete history of your company, too.

If you're speaking to an alumni group to raise funds for

your university, don't throw in a section on the problems of America's high schools.

If you're speaking to the Chamber of Commerce about the need for a new shopping center, don't go off on a tangent about the tax problems of small business.

Get the picture? You're giving a speech, not a dissertation. You can't include every wise thought that's ever crossed your mind.

Remember Voltaire's observation: "The secret of being a bore is to tell everything."

WHAT TO DO IF YOU HAVE NOTHING TO SAY

Suppose—God forbid—that you can't think of anything to talk about? I will give you two anecdotes and two cautions.

> The president of a company called his speechwriter into the room and asked him to write a speech.
> "What about?" the speechwriter asked.
> "Oh," the president said, "about thirty minutes."

Caution: Good speeches do more than fill time. They *say* something.

If you don't know what to say, ask yourself some basic questions about your department, your company, your industry, whatever. Think like a reporter. Dig for good material.

- *Who?*   Who got us into this mess? Who can get us out? Who is really in charge? Who would benefit from this project? Who should get the credit for our success? Who should work on our team? Who will suffer if the merger fails?

- *What?*   What does this situation mean? What actually happened? What went wrong? What is our current status? What do we want to happen? What will the future bring? What is our greatest strength? What is our biggest weakness?

- *Where?*   Where do we go from here? Where can we get help? Where should we cut our budget? Where should we invest? Where should we look for expertise? Where do we want to be in five years? Where can we expand operations? Where will the next problem come from?

- *When?*   When did things start to go wrong? When did things start to improve? When did we first get involved? When will we be ready to handle a new project? When can the company expect to see progress? When will we make money? When will we be able to increase our staff?

- *Why?*   Why did this happen? Why did we get involved? Why did we *not* get involved? Why did we get involved so late? Why do we let this mess continue? Why are we holding this meeting? Why should we stick with this course of action? Why should we continue to be patient? Why did they start that program?

- *How?*   How can we get out of this situation? How did we ever get into it? How can we explain our position? How can we protect ourselves? How should we proceed? How should we spend the money? How will we develop our resources? How can we keep our good reputation? How can we improve our image? How does this program really work?

- *What if?*   What if we could change the tax laws? What if we build another plant? What if the zoning regulations don't change? What if we expand into other subsidiaries? What if deregulation backfires? What if costs keep rising?

These questions should lead you to some interesting ideas.

Need more inspiration? Pick up a trade paper from another field. Read an academic journal from another discipline. Scan a magazine that represents a different political opinion. Look at a foreign publication. Imagine how the readers of any of these publications would think about your subject.

Or, watch a soap opera you've never seen before. Imagine how the characters portrayed would look at your subject.

In short, take inspiration wherever you can get it. The American painter Grant Wood once admitted, "All the really good ideas I ever had came to me while I was milking a cow."

And, mystery writer Agatha Christie confessed she got her best ideas while doing the dishes. So, learn to keep your eyes and ears open.

Take your good ideas wherever you get them.

> Albert Einstein, the story goes, was once asked to speak at Harvard. After a splendid introduction, he walked to the podium, looked at the crowd, paused a long time, and said, "I really have nothing to say." Then he sat down.
>
> The audience just sat in stunned silence. Einstein then stood up again and promised, "When I have something to say, I'll come back."

Caution: Unless your name is Albert Einstein, you probably won't get away with this approach.

If you decide you have absolutely nothing to speak about right now, then decline the invitation. Tell the program director you'd be glad to speak at a later date—when you have more information to share. Then, keep your word.

Remember the wisdom of George Eliot: "Blessed is the man who, having nothing to say, abstains from giving in words evidence of the fact."

Assessing Your Audience

There is a great deal of human nature in people.
—Mark Twain

Before you spend one minute researching your topic, before you write one word of your speech, first analyze your audience. This chapter will give you a list of important questions to ask.

FAMILIARITY WITH THE SUBJECT

How much does the audience already know about the subject? Where did they get their information? How much more do they need or want to know?

ATTITUDES

Why are these people coming to hear you speak? Are they *really* interested in the subject, or did someone (perhaps a boss or a professor) require them to attend? Will they be friendly, hostile, or apathetic?

   A word of caution about "hostile" audiences: Don't be too

quick to assume an audience will be hostile, and never give a speech with a chip on your shoulder.

Even if the audience doesn't agree with your viewpoint, they might appreciate your open-mindedness, your careful reasoning, and your balanced approach.

A word of advice about apathetic audiences: Some people won't be the least bit interested in your subject. Maybe they're in the audience just because they were obligated to attend, or because it was a chance to get out of the office for a while. Granted, *you* may be interested in your subject, but you'll find plenty of people who aren't.

Surprise them. Startle them. Wake them up. Use anecdotes and examples and humor to keep their attention.

PRECONCEIVED NOTIONS

Will the audience have preconceived notions about you and your occupation? *Remember:* People are *never* completely objective. Emotion often overrules reason.

Try to imagine how the audience *feels* about you.

One effective way to make an impression on the audience is to shock them a bit—to confront and shatter their preconceptions. If you surprise their emotions, you may influence their reasoning.

For example: If you are a social worker, the audience may have a preconceived notion of you as a bleeding-heart liberal, someone with no idea of what social work costs the taxpayer.

Shatter this preconception. Talk about the need to cut administrative costs in social agencies. Talk about the need for stiffer penalties for welfare cheats. Talk about the need for personal and professional accountability in the social work profession.

This approach will surprise—and probably impress—them. They will be more likely to *remember* your message.

Appeal to their emotions to influence their thinking.

SIZE

The size of an audience won't affect your subject matter, but it will probably affect your *approach* to the subject matter.

Small groups (say, up to fifteen or twenty people) and large groups have different listening personalities and different psychological orientations. The wise speaker knows how to appeal to the needs of each group.

People in small groups (a board of directors, for example) often know a lot about each other. They can frequently anticipate each other's reactions to new ideas and problems.

People in small groups tend to pay closer attention to you because it's too risky for them to daydream. They may know you, and they may fear being caught off guard by an unexpected question from the podium: "I haven't been involved in the administration of these loans, but I'm sure Paul Smith could tell us about that. Paul, would you give us the latest details?"

You can take advantage of this small-group attentiveness by emphasizing reason and by offering solid information.

People in large audiences *don't* normally know everyone else. It's easier for them to sit back and feel anonymous. It's also easier for them to daydream.

Speeches to a large audience can—indeed, often *should*—be more dramatic, more humorous, more emotional. Rhetorical devices that might seem contrived in a small group are now useful. The larger the crowd, the greater the need for "a good show."

People in large audiences tend to think, "Okay, recognize me, entertain me, inspire me. Make me feel good about myself when I leave here."

Cater to these needs.

Also, there's one other important reason to ask about the size—big or small—of an audience.

Obviously, if you assume several hundred people will attend, you may feel embarrassed and disappointed when only forty show up. On the other hand, consider this awful experience: A spokesperson for a health organization frequently spoke to small groups of nurses. One time she showed up at a convention and learned she had to speak to a couple of hundred nurses in a large auditorium. She didn't know how to use the microphone. Her slide show wasn't bold enough for the new, large space. And she didn't have enough handouts. Is it any wonder she felt overwhelmed and nervous?

AGE

It's important to find out about the *age range* of an audience and to plan your speech accordingly.

Suppose, for example, you must represent your company at a special town meeting. The meeting starts at 7 P.M., and you expect whole families to attend—including parents with young children in tow.

Now, you may *plan* to talk to the homeowners in the audience about the need for new zoning regulations, but you must also be prepared for the pitter-patter of little feet running up and down the aisles and the shrill cries of babies who want to be fed.

Realize that these distractions are inevitable, and that they will probably occur—alas—just when you get to the most critical part of your speech. If you are mentally prepared for these possibilities (and if you have some friendly one-liners ready), you will be less rattled when the disruptions occur.

Or, suppose you're talking to a group of senior citizens. You'll want to pick examples that will reach their particular needs. Keep in mind: As people get older, sex-role lines blur, and couples begin sharing more household chores and other responsibilities—including decision-making. So, make sure your presentation involves everyone.

Or, suppose you're talking to a group of college students. Pace your speech to appeal to young people. Be especially careful with humor. *Remember:* People tend to laugh about things they've had some experience with. So, a younger audience may not laugh at the same anecdotes as an older audience. It's simply a lack of "life experience."

MALE/FEMALE RATIO

Ask in advance about the likely male/female ratio, and use this information to help you prepare appropriate statistics and examples.

Listen to the way New York Governor Mario Cuomo involved women listeners in his State of the State address to the legislature:

> Imagine then, what we could do in this state and in this nation.
>
> Then, someday, not too long from now, another governor could stand here and tell his audience—no, tell *her* audience—that we, the generations that endured depression and global war and the decades-long threat of nuclear destruction, never lost hope and never stopped going forward.

ECONOMIC STATUS

Suppose you speak as a representative of the local electric utility. An affluent, community-minded group might appreciate hearing about your utility's contributions to cultural groups in the area. But people on fixed incomes won't be impressed to learn you give $10,000 each year to the local philharmonic. They would rather hear about specific ways to cut their electric bills or about your utility's efforts to lobby for "energy vouchers" from the government.

Remember: It's all a matter of perspective. Your listeners will be thinking, "What's in this for me?"

EDUCATIONAL BACKGROUND

I once heard an engineer who spoke to all sorts of community groups about his corporation's engineering projects. Unfortunately, he spoke the same way to graduate engineering students as he did to retirees who had no previous experience in the field. You can imagine how well his highly technical speeches went over with the retirees.

Of course, you don't need to change the *point* of your speech. Just talk at a level your audience can understand.

POLITICAL ORIENTATION

Has the group taken an official stand on an important national issue? Did the group actively support a local candidate for office? Does the audience pride itself on being open-minded, or does it take a hard-and-fast view on certain issues?

CULTURAL LIFE

On a Sunday afternoon, would your audience be more likely to visit a museum or take their kids to an amusement park? Would they read *Popular Mechanics, Forbes,* or *Cosmopolitan?*

All of this information will help you understand your audience. When you understand your audience, you'll give a better speech, and you'll have a much easier time with the question-and-answer session.

But, how can you *get* this information about your audience—and get it quickly? Here are nine tips:

1. *Talk with the person who invited you to speak.* If the host is too busy to help, ask for the name and number

of someone who can spend more time with you. Try to talk with this person face-to-face. A telephone conversation is okay, but *don't* rely on a written fact sheet. A fact sheet won't give you insight into the personality of the audience.

2. *Talk with previous speakers.* See what their experiences were like. What worked? What didn't? What would the speakers do differently if they had a second chance?

3. *Talk with someone who will be in the audience.* What are these meetings usually like? Who was the audience's favorite speaker? Least favorite speaker? Why?

4. *Ask their public relations department.* Can they supply an annual report or a newsletter that will give you an idea of the organization's orientation?

5. *Contact the officers of the organization.* (But take their information with the proverbial grain of salt. Officers give "official" information, and rarely provide the candid observations you need.)

6. *Call the reference section of a library.*

7. *If it's an out-of-town speech, ask the local press for some background.*

8. *Use common sense.*

9. *Above all, use a little imagination.* (Curiosity will bring its own rewards. As Einstein advised, "The important thing is not to stop questioning. Curiosity has its own reason for existing.")

AN ADDITIONAL WORD TO THE WISE

It's not smart to give the same speech to different audiences. Why?

- You will eventually get tired of presenting the same material, and your boredom will show.

- No two audiences are alike. Your listeners will have different attitudes, special interests, and pet peeves. A direct proportion exists here: The more you try to lump all of your audiences together, the more they will disregard—and even dislike—you.

- You never know if someone in the audience might have heard you give the identical speech somewhere else.

Improbable? Think about this embarrassing situation. One Monday morning at the Waldorf-Astoria, a minister pronounced the benediction before a breakfast meeting of the American Newspaper Publishers Association.

Later in the day, he returned to the Waldorf-Astoria to give the blessing at an Associated Press luncheon. It was—you guessed it—the same prayer, and listeners who attended both meetings were quick to pick up the repeated phrases.

Even worse, the *New York Times* was quick to pick up the story, and ran it under the headline "Invoking the Familiar."

Funny? Sure—as long as it happened to someone else and not to you.

THREE

Where and When Will You Speak?

✳ ────────────────────────────────────

Precaution must be taken in advance.
—Japanese proverb

────────────────────────────────────

After you've determined what your audience will be like, the next step (yes, you should do this before you head to the library and before you put pen to paper) is to consider where and when you will give your speech.

WHERE

Let's start with the basics. Where, *exactly,* will you give the speech?

- In the training center of a large corporation?

- In a university auditorium?

- In a high school classroom?

- In a hotel conference room?

- In a gymnasium?

- In a restaurant?
- On an outdoor platform?

Does it make any difference? Yes.

Plan a Speech That's Appropriate to the Setting

For example:

- If you're speaking on an outdoor platform (as is common at graduations), be sensitive to the weather. Know how to "wrap up" your speech in a hurry if a June thunderstorm cuts you short.

- If you must speak in a large banquet hall, have some one-liners ready for the inevitable moments when waiters interrupt your speech to serve coffee and drown out your words with the clatter of dishes.

- If you'll be in a hotel conference room, bring along some signs reading, "Quiet please—Meeting in progress." Post these signs on the doors to alert people passing through the corridor.

If you've never seen the location, ask the program host for a rough sketch of the room. How big is the area? Where will you stand? Where will the audience sit? Are the chairs movable? "Seeing" all this on paper first will help you feel more comfortable when you actually speak there.

You might even be able to tie the setting into the theme of your speech. Consider this opening by Gerald Greenwald, vice chairman of Chrysler, to the Society of Automotive Engineers banquet in Detroit:

> This is also the first time in my life that I've given a speech atop a lazy Susan! Leave it to engineers, in the city of wheels, to put *the speaker* on a wheel!

In the Middle Ages, as some of you may know, a wheel like the one I'm standing on could have had quite a bit of significance. In medieval allegory, spinnings of "the wheel"—also known as the "wheel of fortune"—represented the uncertainties of fate. If the wheel spun against you, you were in for bad luck. If it spun in your favor, you had good luck.

Today I think we are all wondering what the next spin of the fortune wheel will bring this great industry of ours.

WHEN

Again, the basics. When, *exactly,* will you give the speech?

- At a breakfast meeting?
- At a mid-morning seminar?
- Just before lunch?
- During lunch?
- After lunch, before people return to work?
- As part of a mid-afternoon panel?
- At 4 P.M., as the final speaker in the day's seminar?
- At 9 P.M., as the after-dinner speaker?
- At 11 P.M., as the last in a string of after-dinner speakers?

Plan a Speech That Suits the Time of Day

Use your imagination. Always look at the event from the audience's perspective. What will be on *their* minds?

For example:

- You must be especially brief and succinct at a breakfast meeting. Why? Because your breakfast meeting forced the audience to get up an hour or two early. And because they still face a whole day's work ahead of them. If your speech is not organized and clear and concise—and if they can't get to their offices on time—they will resent you.

- If you speak on a mid-afternoon panel, find out whether you'll speak first or last. Panel presentations run notoriously behind schedule, and the last speaker often feels "squeezed" for time. Be realistic, and be prepared to give a shortened presentation, if necessary.

- If you speak after a banquet (perhaps to celebrate a retirement), know that the audience has been eating and drinking for several hours. They will be in a good mood. They will want to *stay* in a good mood. Don't ruin their evening with an overly long, overly serious speech.

Should You Request a Particular Time Slot?

Yes, if it will improve the effect of your speech.

Suppose, for example, you learn that you're scheduled to speak after a series of award presentations. You suspect, and rightly so, that the audience will be restless after hearing all those thank-you speeches. What should you do?

Be assertive. Let the program host know that you're willing to listen to the award presentations, but that you're not willing to follow them.

If you are showing a movie or slides and will require a darkened room, ask to speak mid-morning or mid-afternoon. Avoid darkened rooms immediately after lunch or dinner. They are conducive to sleep—and the last thing you want is to have your speech interrupted by snores.

A Caution About Out-of-Town Conferences

Know what you're up against. People who travel to a conference in sunny Florida in the middle of January aren't going there just to hear your speech. And people who go to a conference in Las Vegas may not even want to hear your speech at all.

Consider Hubert H. Humphrey's advice for addressing restless audiences:

"You say, 'Buzz-buzz-buzz-buzz-buzz—Franklin Delano Roosevelt! Buzz-buzz-buzz-buzz-buzz—Harry S. Truman! Buzz-buzz-buzz-buzz-buzz—John Fitzgerald Kennedy!' And then you get the hell out of there before they start throwing rolls at each other."

How to Research a Speech

❋ ─────────────────────────────

Facts are ventriloquists' dummies. Sitting on a man's
knee, they may be made to utter words of wisdom;
elsewhere they say nothing, or talk nonsense.
—Aldous Huxley

───────────────────────────────

Now that you've determined the nature of your audience and
considered where and when you will speak, the next step is to
gather information for your speech. But don't rush off to the
library yet. Instead, just sit down and *think*.

USE YOUR HEAD

Your best information source is always *your own head*. Ask
yourself, "What do I *already* know about this subject?" Then
jot down your thoughts.

Don't worry about organization at this point. Just make
some rough notes. Write down important facts, opinions, examples—whatever information you already know. Let your
notes sit for a day or two, if possible. Then review them.

Now, begin to look for *specific* information in the form of statistics, quotations, examples, definitions, comparisons, and contrasts.

If you don't have enough specifics or enough *variety* of specifics, do some research and get them. Again, start your research close to home and branch out as needed:

- Go through your files.

- Leaf through magazines related to the subject.

- Consult with friends and business associates.

- Call up a specialist in the field and ask for a comment.

- Introduce yourself to a reference librarian, explain your speech assignment, and ask for resources.

MAKE GOOD USE OF THE LIBRARY

Reference librarians are invaluable to any speechwriter. Absolutely invaluable. They know their way around a library and can save you countless hours of time and frustration.

Many reference librarians even handle inquiries over the telephone. If this service is available at your local library, keep the telephone number handy.

If you expect to give many speeches during your career, become friendly with a reference librarian. Take a reference librarian to lunch. It's a worthwhile investment in your career.

Another worthwhile investment? Become familiar with some basic reference books. I've included a list of basic reference books at the end of this. They will help you write better speeches—and they will help you do it faster.

These reference books are widely available in public libraries, but if you write a lot of speeches you will want to buy some of them for your personal library.

WHAT TO LEAVE OUT

As the speaker, you're in control: *You* get to choose the precise topic. You also get to decide what information stays and what information goes. What *not* to say is just as important as what *to* say.

Leave out:

- irrelevant details

- boring details

- any information you can't verify

- anything you wouldn't want to see quoted in print the next day

- anything you wouldn't want to be reminded of next year

APPROACH THE TOPIC FROM THE AUDIENCE'S PERSPECTIVE

Your audience can understand your subject only by relating it to their own ideas and problems and experiences. So, approach the subject from *their* perspective, not *your* perspective.

For example, don't just complain about your industry's problems. Even if you have some legitimate complaints, your audience will probably not care. They have enough problems of their own.

Instead, relate *your* concerns to *their* concerns. Find the emotional "hook" that will help the audience understand your message.

Talk about audience *benefits*. Show how the audience would benefit if your industry could solve its problems. Would the audience save money? Save time? Be healthier? Be happier?

Approach the topic from their perspective, and you'll be more effective. It's a fact: Audiences tend to trust—and to like—speakers who show a real understanding of them.

HOW TO USE STATISTICS FOR IMPACT

Some people think statistics are boring. These people have not heard the right statistics.

Statistics can be downright interesting, *if* you:

1. *Make the statistics seem real to your audience.* Try, "While we're sitting here for an hour and debating the value of sex education in the schools, 'x number' of teenage girls will give birth to illegitimate children."

    Or, "While you're watching your favorite TV show tonight, forty-five people will call the national cocaine hotline to ask for help. Could one of them be *your* child?"

2. *Explain what your statistics mean.* When the Southern Newspaper Publishers Association talks to community groups about the dangers of illiteracy, they try to put the numbers in perspective:

    In 1929, University of Chicago President Robert Hutchins said, "To destroy the Western tradition of independent thought, it is not necessary to burn the books. All we have to do is leave them unread for a couple of generations."

    Here we are . . . years later . . . and it's not only books being left unread. It's newspapers. It's job applications. It's instruction manuals. It's even warning labels on medicine bottles.

    Today, in the U.S. there are 23 million adults who cannot read. They cannot read or write or compute well enough to compete in today's job market—much less perpetuate the tradition of independent thought.

3. *Put statistics in simple terms.* Don't just say that your senator will mail "x" million items to his constituents this year. Instead, explain that this amounts to about three deliveries to every mailbox in his district. Everyone who has a mailbox can relate to that statistic.

4. *Round off the numbers.* Say "almost one million customers," not "997,755 customers." Make it easy for the audience to *hear* and *remember* your statistics.

5. *Use numbers sparingly.* Audiences cannot absorb more than a couple of numbers at a time. If you use too many statistics, you will lose your listeners.

6. *Be graphic.* Try to paint a picture with numbers. Say, "It's as long as four football fields." Or, "The stack of papers would be as tall as the bank building across the street." Or, "You'd have to dig a hole big enough to hide a supertanker."

My point is: Let your audience *see* your numbers by using real-life examples.

When Senator Donald Riegle, Jr., rebutted President Reagan's budget message, he held up a copy of *Newsweek* and said:

"Here is the current issue of *Newsweek*—most of it deals with unemployment. Here is a picture of the Wilk family from Hamtramck, Michigan. If every unemployed family had one page in this magazine, it would take eleven million pages. It would be a stack as high as seven football fields. And yet we're told to stay on this course?"

Or, listen to an excerpt of a speech by FBI Director William Sessions to the Commonwealth Club of California:

"Just how much is a hundred pounds of heroin? Well, let me describe it this way: Even just twenty-five pounds of high-quality heroin is enough to overdose every man, woman, and child in the city of San Francisco."

7. *Do not apologize for using statistics.* Inexperienced speakers often say, "I hate to bore you with statistics, *but . . ."* After this apology, they proceed to bore their audiences with poorly chosen and poorly used statistics.

Avoid this pitfall. If you follow the guidelines in this chapter, your statistics will *not* be boring. They will, in fact, add a lot of interest to your speech.

HOW TO USE QUOTATIONS

Audiences love quotations, *if* you:

1. *Use some variety.* If you're speaking about productivity, for example, don't just quote the U.S. Department of Labor. Use a variety of sources. Try:

- Abraham Lincoln ("My father taught me to work; he did not teach me to love it.")

- Robert Frost ("The world is full of willing people; some willing to work, the rest willing to let them.")

- The Bible ("The harvest truly is plenteous, but the labourers are few.")

- The president of a local union

- The manager of a large personnel department

- An industrial psychologist

- An anonymous commentator ("People come up to me and say, 'Yours is the best-run factory in the United States.' And that makes me feel great. But I know our productivity will start to decline if we ever become too proud or too careless.")

2. *Avoid lengthy or complicated quotations.* Keep quotations short. Cut or paraphrase any "slow parts."

3. *Blend the quotation into the text.* Never say "quote . . . unquote." Instead, pause a moment and let your voice emphasize the quotation. Listen to this skillful use of a quotation by Lynne Cheney, Chairman of the National Endowment for the Humanities:

> "The humanities are alive and well. . . . Recently, millions of Americans—record numbers of them— watched Ken Burns's remarkable documentary, *The Civil War*—a film for which I am very proud to note that the National Endowment for the Humanities provided *major* funding. I understand that Brandon Tartikoff, Chairman of the NBC Entertainment Group, was somewhat dismayed when he heard about *The Civil War* ratings. 'It used to be just cable and Fox,' Tartikoff said. 'Now I have to worry about PBS?' "

4. *Appear comfortable with the quotation.* Never quote anybody unless you're sure you can pronounce the name right. I once heard a speaker quote "the well-known German writer, Goethe." Unfortunately, he pronounced the name as "Goath"—and the quotation just fell flat.

5. *Use quotations judiciously.* A speech should reflect *your* thoughts and expertise, so don't quote dozens of other people. In a fifteen-minute speech, you can probably use two or three quotations. *Remember:* The impact of your quotations will decline sharply as their number grows.

HOW TO USE DEFINITIONS

What do you mean when you speak about "liquidity problems"? About "decreasing profit margins"? About "a captive finance company"?

1. *Define your terms in everyday words.* Avoid "dictionary" definitions. "According to Webster, . . ." is a phrase that sounds feeble and amateurish.

2. *Try a definition with a light touch.* You might want to ask a six-year-old for a definition of "management compensation" or "gun control" or "inflation." You'll get some amusing definitions that could add interest to your speech.

HOW TO USE COMPARISONS AND CONTRASTS

Use everyday comparisons to which people can easily relate.

When Leo Durocher was manager of the Brooklyn Dodgers, he was booed for pulling a pitcher out late in a close game. Afterward, a reporter asked him how he felt about the crowd's reaction. Durocher's comparison? "Baseball is like church. Many attend. Few understand."

More recently, T. Boone Pickens, the Texas oil baron and corporate takeover specialist, made this observation about corporate democracy (or, lack thereof):

"Even most of the Eastern bloc countries now have elections that are more democratic than those of America's publicly owned corporations."

HOW TO USE EXAMPLES

Examples can be interesting. Unfortunately, they can also be misleading. President Reagan once cited the example of a "welfare queen" who used false names to collect multiple benefits. However, he failed to show that this example was *representative.* He failed to prove that the "welfare queen" was typical of people who get government aid. In short, he failed to use an example properly.

Always remember: An example is *not* proof. If you use an example, make sure it gives the audience a fair picture of the situation. Otherwise, you will lose your credibility.

SOME FINAL THOUGHTS ABOUT RESEARCH

Sophisticated listeners will question the source of your information. Make sure the source is *reputable* and *appropriate* for your particular audience.

Also, be sure to use a *mixture* of material in your speech—maybe one or two quotations, an example, a couple of bold statistics, and a comparison. This variety will make your speech more interesting and more credible.

Be aware: Some people just don't assimilate certain types of information. "Numbers people" may consider anecdotes "frivolous" or "invalid." "People people" may mistrust statistics, preferring to receive their information in anecdotal form.

Use a combination of techniques to get your message across.

As Bette Midler describes the way she puts together an effective show, "I always try to balance the light with the heavy—a few tears for the human spirit in with the sequins and the fringes." That same balance can work to the advantage of anyone trying to gather research for a speech. The *variety* can prove powerful—and create a more memorable speech.

FIVE

Writing the Speech

Planning to write is not writing. Outlining . . . researching
. . . talking to people about what you're doing . . . none
of that is writing. Writing is writing.
—E. L. Doctorow

All right. Enough thinking, enough planning, enough researching. Now's the time to sit down and write.

What do you have to do to write a good speech? Two things:

1. Make it simple.
2. Make it short.

What do you have to do to write a *great* speech?

1. Make it simpler.
2. Make it shorter.

In this chapter, I'll tell you how to make your speech simple and easy to understand. In the next chapter, I'll show you specific techniques to make it short—and memorable.

These two chapters are the guts of the book. Read them carefully. Reread them with a pencil in your hand. Mark the hell out of them. Because they tell you everything this professional speechwriter knows about writing speeches.

THE NEVER-FAIL FORMULA

Here's the formula for a successful speech. It works every time.

- Tell them what you're going to tell them.
- Tell them.
- Tell them what you've told them.

TELL THEM WHAT YOU'RE GOING TO TELL THEM: THE OPENING

I won't mince words. The opening is the toughest part. If you don't hook your listeners within the first thirty seconds, your cause is probably lost.

Start with a "grabber"—an anecdote, a startling statistic, a quotation, a personal observation, a literary, historical, or biblical allusion. Use whatever it takes to get the audience's attention. Give them a good taste of what's to come.

It can be risky to begin a speech with a joke. If it falls flat, you're off to a terrible start, so don't use a joke unless you are *absolutely* sure you can deliver it well. Even then, use a joke only if it's short and if it relates to the topic of the speech.

Never, *never,* open by saying something like, "I heard a really funny story today. It doesn't have anything to do with my speech, but at least it'll give you a good laugh."

Instead, try one of these opening techniques:

Praise the Audience

Here's how Dr. R. Malcolm Overbey, of the American Dental Association, opened his keynote address to the Hinman Dental Meeting:

When you're going to a place in Washington, D.C., that probably holds more history than any other building in America, you don't have to say you're going to the Smithsonian Institution. You say you're going to the *Smithsonian,* and everybody knows what you're talking about.

If you're taking a trip on the fastest commercial jet ever built, you really don't need to point that out to people. As a matter of fact, you don't even have to say you'll be flying. All you have to do is say you'll be taking the Concorde, and everybody knows what you're talking about.

If you're going to a one-of-a kind dental meeting, put together by a one-of-a-kind group of people, there's no need to tell anybody in dentistry that you're going to the Hinman *Dental Meeting.* Just say the *Hinman,* and they know you're going to one of the best.

Try Some Self-Depreciating Humor

Here's how Peter Walters, chairman of British Petroleum, disarmed the audience with some opening humor:

"Two old ladies were walking around a somewhat over-crowded English country churchyard, and they came upon a tombstone on which was the inscription: 'Here lies John Smith, an oilman and an honest man.'

'Good heavens!' said one lady to the other. 'Isn't it awful that they had to put two people in the same grave!' "

Make a Reference to the Date

When Paul O'Brien, president of New England Telephone, spoke to the Vermont School Board Association, he referred to the significance of the date:

Today, as some of you might know, is the day the National Council of Teachers of English presents the annual "Doublespeak" Awards. And, even the best of speeches are filled with their share of doublespeak.

I'm sure you know what "doublespeak" is. Or, at least you know it when you hear it.

Doublespeak's that globbledygook rhetoric that just doesn't ring true . . . sterile language and mumbo jumbo designed to take something bad and try to make it sound like something good.

Businesses are frequent users of doublespeak. Layoffs are made in the name of "downsizing," "corporate rightsizing," or as a way to "enhance shareholder value."

For instance, airlines don't worry about how many bags they lose; they worry about the "misconnect rate."

Sackers at the grocery store are "packaging agents," and the guy who changes your oil at the gas station is an "automotive fluid maintenance technician."

And then he promised his audience that his speech would contain *no* doublespeak—just straight talk about his subject.

Ask Some Questions

Questions are an effective way to involve an audience. Listen to this opener by Fred Halperin, chairman of the International Association of Business Communicators Research Foundation:

Let me start by asking you a few questions. How many of you would say that you practice excellent communication for your organization?

Now, let's say your communications department costs your organization $100,000 a year. What kind of return on investment would you say your department gives your organization? One hundred percent would be $100,000; that means your value pays for your cost. Would it be less than a hundred percent? More?

Okay, now how would your CEO answer that question?

Use a Lighthearted Story to Illustrate Some Statistics

Remarks from William Link, executive vice president of the Prudential Insurance Company of America, before the Commonwealth Club of California:

> This year Americans will spend close to $700 billion on health care—almost twelve percent of GNP. Even adjusted for inflation, that's twice what we spent in 1965. Almost triple what we spent in 1950. . . .
>
> An old story pretty well describes why our health-care costs are out of control.
>
> A patient comes to see a highly respected doctor for an examination. After three days of intensive tests, the patient gets the bill.
>
> He rushes back into the doctor's office and says, "What, are you crazy, Doc? I can't pay that. Two thousand dollars. My goodness."
>
> The doctor says, "All right, in your case, just give me half."
>
> "Half? I can't even pay half."
>
> "Well, what portion of the bill do you think you can pay?"
>
> "Not a penny. I'm a poor man."
>
> "With all due respect," sighs the doctor, "why did you come to me—one of the greatest specialists of our time?"
>
> "Listen, doc," the man replies, "when it comes to my health, money is no object."
>
> Americans want the best care money can buy, but we are shocked when we get the bills. Those bills will only get worse as our population ages and medical technology grows more complex.

Use Imagery

Listen to the way Lloyd Reuss, president of General Motors, creates a picturesque metaphor to get the attention of his audience, the Mid-American Society of Automotive Engineers:

> It's important to get together and talk with you every now and then, just because we're living in a time of such rapid and exciting

change. The guy who said you can never step into the same river twice—because the constant flow makes it a different river—ought to be around today to see what we've got: a swift and powerful current, with lots of twists and turns, and plenty of white water. But I think it's great—and so should you . . . because it all creates, if you'll pardon the expression, a whole raft of new challenges for engineers.

Tell a Story

Here's how John Jacob, CEO of the National Urban League, addressed the American Assembly of Collegiate Schools of Business in St. Louis, Missouri:

> The last time I attended a meeting of educators I heard a story about a fellow who returned to his alma mater to visit his son, who was now a student there.
>
> When he discovered that his son was taking a course with a professor who once taught him, he sat in on the class. Well, that day the professor gave a surprise test, and to this fellow's amazement, he noticed that every question was on the test the professor had given thirty years earlier.
>
> When the class ended, the fellow was very upset and asked the professor how he could give the same test he had given so long ago.
>
> "Ah, yes," the professor answered. "I give the same questions, but now the answers are different."
>
> Times have changed.

Cite Your Professional Credentials—or Your Personal Credentials—or, Even Better, Both

E. James Morton, CEO of John Hancock Mutual Life Insurance Company, spoke to the National Conference on Work and Family Issues and created a strong rapport with this opening:

Well, my instructions were to be as provocative and visionary as I can. . . . I am, by training, an actuary. A common definition is that an actuary is someone who didn't have enough personality to be an accountant. Provocativeness and vision are not normally in our bag of tricks. But, we do know a little bit about demographics and how to project trends, so let me do the best I can per instructions.

I might also add, on a personal basis, that my own situation does give me a fairly broad range of experience in family matters.

I have a ninety-year-old mother; three daughters whose ages are forty-one, twenty-six, and eight; a nine-month-old grandson, and a baby-boomer wife whose mother is a World War II Icelandic war bride, and who lives in another city to which I commute on weekends.

So I believe that I can relate closely to practically any demographic or family situation that anyone can bring up.

Openings for Special Circumstances

If you're making a return engagement . . .

Let the audience know how pleased you are to address them again.

Donald Coonley, Chief National Bank Examiner, took this lighthearted approach when he addressed the Urban Bankers Forum:

To be invited twice to speak to the same group is a great honor. A return performance is not always automatic. And Winston Churchill once used this fact to his advantage.

Churchill received an invitation from George Bernard Shaw to one of his opening plays back in the early 1900s. Shaw's note read: "Enclosed are two tickets to the first-night performance of a play of mine. Bring a friend—if you have one."

Not to be outdone, Churchill shot back this reply: "Dear G.B.S., I thank you very much for the invitation and the tickets. Unfortunately, I am engaged on that night, but could I have tickets for the second performance—if there is one?"

I am happy and honored that there is—for me—a second performance before this group.

If you are a substitute speaker . . .

So, you're a last-minute invitee? Get it out in the open, and move on.

When Richard Merrill, as executive vice president of the Prudential Insurance Company of America, served as a substitute speaker, he used this straightforward opening:

"Thank you for that warm reception. And let me extend Bob Winter's sincere apologies for not being able to keep his date with you today. Only a very unexpected and significant business problem could have kept him from being here."

After these few explanatory sentences, he then moved on to his topic, America's sick health-care system.

If you are speaking out of town . . .

Avoid this all-too-common opening: "It's great being here in Cincinnati/Philadelphia/Walla Walla."

The first thing your audience wants to know is "Why?" "Why on earth," they're saying to themselves, "are you so thrilled to be here in Cincinnati/Philadelphia/Walla Walla?"

Were you born here? Did you go to college here? Did you start your first job here? If so, then *tell* the audience. They'll appreciate the personal connection.

Here's how Robert Scherer, retired Chairman of the Board of the Georgia Power Company, opened a speech to the Greater Rome (Georgia) Chamber of Commerce:

"I can't begin to tell you what a pleasure it is to be back here in Rome. I feel just like I've come home, and in a very real sense I have. I spent some of the happiest years of my life and the most rewarding times of my career right here in Rome. And as I return, I see you're still enjoying the best of *both* worlds. You live in a dynamic, growing community with all the charm of small-town living—a perfect mix."

If you're the last to speak . . .

Keep it brief, and make it lively. *Remember:* The poor audience has been sitting there listening to speech after speech—each probably more tedious than the one before! So, give them a break, and let them end on an up beat.

One time, George Bernard Shaw had to follow a series of speakers, and he took this approach:

After he was introduced and the applause subsided, he simply said, "Ladies and gentlemen, the subject may not be exhausted, but we are." And, with that summation, he sat down.

There might be a lesson in that.

Some Cautions About Beginning a Speech

It's not necessary—or even desirable—to begin with: "Good evening, ladies and gentlemen." Greetings like this are really just fillers. Skip them. Jump right in with the first line of your speech.

The same goes with most introductory *thank you*'s. They can sound pretty feeble, and feeble is not the way to begin a speech. Whatever you do, avoid trite openings. Almost every run-of-the-mill (read: boring) speech begins with something like, "It's such a wonderful pleasure to be here today." Who is this speaker trying to kid? Since when is speechmaking such a pleasure?

Everyone knows that giving a speech is hard work. Most people would rather do *anything* than stand up and give a speech.

Don't flash a phony smile and open with a glib line. Audiences are quick to spot insincerity. And they're slow to forgive you for it.

If you're really enthusiastic about giving your speech, it will show in your content and delivery. You won't have to fake it with flowery openings.

TELL THEM: THE BODY

> Organize is what you do before you do something, so that
> when you do it, it's not all mixed up.
> —Christopher Robin in A. A. Milne's *Winnie the Pooh*

Inexperienced speechwriters want to say everything, and that's where they make their first mistake. Focus your material, and limit the number of points you make. If you concentrate on one central idea, your audience will stand a better chance of understanding you.

Wait a minute. Are you saying to yourself, "But my topic is so important, I've *got* to get everything across"?

Don't get carried away with your own importance.

If you try to say *everything,* your audience will come away with *nothing.* It's as simple as that.

No matter what your speech is about, you must limit, focus, and organize your material. There are lots of ways to do this. Use whatever method works best for you.

Chronological Order

Try dividing your material into time units—from past to present to future—or whatever pattern seems to fit. This method can be effective because it *connects* everything. For example: If a new tax law adversely affects your company, review or predict its effects at ten-year intervals. Start with the present, perhaps, and show how the law hurts your business today. Then go back ten years—before the law went into effect—and show how your company was better off. Take the offensive law ten years into the future and predict how it will hurt your company then. Will you have to lay off employees? Will you have to reduce your contributions to local cultural groups? Will you have to stop production on a new plant?

Show how historical changes affect the quality of people's lives. If possible, show how these changes affect the quality of your *audience's* lives.

Cause and Effect

Did you start an employee program that has producea positive benefits throughout the company? Then say, "I'd like to tell you about our new Employee Suggestion Plan. It's a success, and it has improved productivity in all seven departments of our company."

Did something go wrong with your marketing plan and cause problems elsewhere? Use that cause-and-effect relationship to organize your speech.

Was your transportation section able to reduce its gasoline costs this year? Tell what caused that improvement: better maintenance, more efficient routes, etc.

Numerical Order

You can go from the highest to the lowest number, or from the lowest to the highest.

Suppose you want to show how your volume of oil production has increased. Look at the numbers as part of an escalating trend. Relate them to specific events so the audience can see *why* your oil production went up.

Suppose you want to show how theft has been reduced in your distribution department. Explain to your audience *why* those numbers went down.

Always relate numbers to *human* events. That's the only way they will make sense to your audience—which will, presumably, be composed largely of humans.

Problem-Solution Approach

Is there something wrong with your tuition aid program? Then tell your audience about the problem and propose some solutions.

Do this with candor and honesty. If you have a problem, bring it out into the open. Chances are, your audience *already* knows about the problem. Admit it honestly, and you'll come across as credible.

Also, if you think your proposed solutions will be difficult, say so. No one likes a snow job.

Geographical Order

Organizing a national sales conference? Start by reporting sales in the eastern districts and work west.

Reviewing the physical expenditures of your company's plants? Start with the northern ones and work south.

Evaluating the productivity of your bank's branches? Take it neighborhood by neighborhood.

Alphabetical Order

Why not? This certainly is easy for the audience to follow. And there are times when alphabetical order may be the only way to organize your information—lists of committees or departments, for example.

Psychological Order

Sometimes it's best to organize your speech based on the psychological needs of the audience.

What will they find most acceptable? Most important? Most interesting? Put that first.

Think about the attitudes your audience may have. If you expect them to be hostile or resistant, then ease slowly into your speech. Begin on common ground and put your most acceptable ideas up front. Don't expect to convince everyone of everything. There's usually a limit to the controversial ideas that any audience can accept.

Some sensitive areas in the business world (pro/antinuclear power and labor/management confrontations, for example) *require* attention to psychological order.

Transitions

No matter which method you use, make sure you follow the order *smoothly*. Do not get sidetracked. If you say something like, "But before I do that, I'd like to give you a little background on the history of our firm," you're heading for trouble.

Keep things moving. Use strong transitions to help the audience follow your ideas. Try such transitional phrases as:

- Moving on to the second territory . . .
- Now let's take a look at . . .
- So much for supply, but what about demand?
- Switching now to the western division . . .
- Looking ahead to the next five years . . .
- Now let me shift gears for a moment . . .
- But to look at it another way . . .
- In addition . . .

Special Circumstances

How to Handle a Crisis

Your company faces a serious crisis, and it's your job to explain the issue to the employees.

1st: Present several undeniable facts that show the seriousness of the situation. Do this *up front*. Be sure to do it without exaggeration, or the audience will suspect your motives.

2nd: Explore possible solutions to the crisis: tighter budget control, increased productivity, etc.

3rd: Solicit the ideas and support of *everyone* in the company to make the program work. Let them know exactly what you expect from them.

Caution: Don't treat every situation like a crisis, or you will lose credibility. You are entitled to one, maybe two, crises in your career. No more.

If you try to turn every situation into a crisis, your audience will see you as the little boy (or girl) who cried wolf once too often. They won't bother to listen anymore.

How to admit you've made a mistake

Have you shown an error in judgment? Made a foolish decision? Chosen the wrong person for a job? Backed the losing team? Pursued a dangerous course?

No sense in hiding your role. Everyone already knows. So, bring your mistake out in the open, clear the air, and set the stage to move on.

Listen to the way President Reagan addressed the nation on the Iran-Contra affair:

Now what should happen when you make a mistake is this: You take your knocks, you learn your lessons, and then you move on. That's the healthiest way to deal with a problem. . . .

You know, by the time you reach my age, you've made plenty of mistakes, and if you've lived your life properly, you learn. You put things in perspective. You pull your energies together. You change. You go forward.

My fellow Americans, I have a great deal that I want to accomplish with you and for you over the next two years, and, the Lord willing, that's exactly what I intend to do. Good night and God bless you.

How to address a person or group who sometimes disagrees with you

When President Bush appeared at a fund-raising event for Representative Claudine Schneider, he faced a dilemma. Ms. Schneider was one of several Republican women who had been urging the President to ease his opposition to abortion rights. How could he deal with her open disapproval regarding his antiabortion stance?

He used diplomacy as he alluded to her disagreements with him and with Republican party leadership.

"Sometimes, pace-setters run alone. Sometimes Claudine disagrees with her party. But, with Claudine, I can always bank on one thing. I always know exactly where she stands—right by her principles."

How to handle an emotional moment

Trying to deal with a tragedy? A community crisis? A painful situation? Be realistic. Your emotions may overcome you, so it's wise to think about how you might handle yourself *before* you begin your speech.

Perhaps this real-life example will prove both inspirational and instructional:

When President Bush paid tribute to the forty-seven dead crew members of the battleship *Iowa,* he said, "They came from Hidalgo, Texas, and Cleveland, Ohio; from Tampa, Florida, and Costa Mesa, California. They came to the Navy as strangers, served the Navy as shipmates and friends, and left the Navy as brothers in eternity."

An audience of three thousand mourners listened as the President's words soon gave way to emotion. His voice cracked when he said, "Your men are under a different command now, one that knows no rank, only love; knows no danger, only peace." And then, tears filled President Bush's eyes.

Apparently, the President feared he would lose control of his emotions, so he wisely dropped the final lines of his address, managed to say, "May God bless them," swallowed hard, turned abruptly, and left the lectern.

Later on, both President and Mrs. Bush walked among the aisles of mourners, comforting them and embracing them. During difficult moments, Mrs. Bush wept openly. President Bush managed to keep his tears in check—but he prudently kept a handkerchief in his hand, just in case he needed it.

How to express disappointment

Suppose some big plan failed—and failed publicly. Now it's your responsibility to tell the audience why the old plan failed and to make some new proposals.

Beware. The audience may be extremely sensitive about the issue and they may fear being blamed for the whole mess.

Reassure them that the original plan was a good one. Say it made sense based on the information available at the time it was conceived. Say no one could have predicted the sudden changes in events that caused the original plan to fail.

Once the audience feels safe from any finger-pointing, they will be receptive to your message.

State the problem clearly and objectively. Admit disappointment, but don't dwell on past failures. Let your emphasis be on a new plan that's based on new data.

How to turn a negative into a positive

Did your fund-raising campaign fail to meet its goals? Then find a way to turn those negative facts into a positive truth.

As Frank Lloyd Wright put it, "The truth is more important than the facts." If some of your facts are disappointing, try to find a larger, more positive truth.

How to turn your company's small size into a big asset

Are you a David doing business in a world of Goliaths? Capitalize on your unique strengths.

Listen to the clever way Joanne Davis, president of OMON: New York, Ltd., positions her small but dynamic advertising agency when she pursues new clients:

I will tell you about some interesting differences and similarities between big-agency new business and small-agency new business.

First, what I was selling in a large agency is poles apart from what I'm selling now. At a large agency, I was selling depth, and resources, and media clout. I had lots of people to draw upon, and relevant and diverse experience and talent. With hundreds and hundreds of employees, I was able to find fast staffing. . . .

Now, OMON's a very different kettle of fish.

As a small agency, I can promise that the owners and founders will be doing the work—that the people in the new business pitch will not disappear mysteriously once the business is won. I can brag about our creative strengths.

The agency reel I show is not the output of hundreds, but the impressive output of a handful of creatives who will actually work on the prospect's account. We may be lacking gray hair, but we have the asset of youth and energy for the long haul.

One Final Point

Double-check your speech to make sure that if you say "first," you follow it with a "second." Otherwise your audience—and maybe even you—will become hopelessly lost.

Be careful, though, not to overuse the "first, second, third" references. They can be boring.

TELL THEM WHAT YOU TOLD THEM: THE CONCLUSION

Now's the time to sum it up—simply and directly. No new thoughts, please. You must avoid the temptation to "stick in" any additional points at the end. It's too late for that.

Your conclusion may be the only thing the audience remembers, so make it memorable.

Here are some effective ways to end a speech:

Use Compelling Imagery

Here's how Thomas Kuhn, president of the Edison Electric Institute, wrapped up his speech at EEI's annual conference:

> The time may come when we will be able to make anything from anything else, given more energy. And we *will* have enough energy, if we don't lose our faith in human ingenuity.
>
> Energy, efficiency, and ingenuity. They are the hope for the future, just as surely as they are the foundation of the past. This is our story. It is a story of progress and growth, a story we must tell others.
>
> The road we travel is a long one; it stretches all the way back from the present to that first energy-using ancestor, and on ahead to the far horizon. I don't know what's beyond that horizon, but I'll bet on this: We will meet it head-on, with a fire in our bellies, a wind in our sails, steam up, and a full charge!

Share Your Personal Philosophy

When Harvey Mackay, best-selling author of *Swim with the Sharks without Being Eaten Alive,* gave the MBA commencement address at Penn State University, he created a strong emotional appeal by sharing this story from his boyhood:

> When I was a kid, my father knew a guy named Bernie who had started out his career with a vegetable stand, worked hard all his life, and eventually became wealthy as a fruit and vegetable wholesaler.
>
> Every summer, when the first good watermelons came in, Dad would take me down to Bernie's warehouse and we'd have a feast. Bernie would choose a couple of watermelons just in from the field, crack them open, and hand each of us a big piece. Then, with Bernie taking the lead, we'd eat only the heart of the watermelon—the reddest, juiciest, most perfect part—and throw the rest away.
>
> My father never made a lot of money. We were raised to clean our plates and not waste food. Bernie was my father's idea of a rich man. I always thought it was because he'd been such a success in business.

It was years before I realized my father admired Bernie's "rich-ness" because he knew how to stop work in the middle of a summer day, sit down with his friends, and spend time eating the heart of the watermelon.

Being rich isn't about money. Being rich is a state of mind. Some of us, no matter how much money we have, will never be free enough to take the time to stop and eat the heart of the watermelon. And some of us will be rich without ever being more than a paycheck ahead of the game. . . .

From my standpoint, that's what it's all about. . . .

Never stop learning.

Believe in yourself, even when no one else does.

Find a way to make a difference, and . . .

Eat the heart of the watermelon.

Then go out and make your own tracks in the snow.

Tie Your Theme to an Anniversary

Vice President Dan Quayle once addressed the American Bar Association on the need for reform in America's legal sys-tem—a topic, one might suppose, that would ruffle more than a few feathers at an ABA convention.

Quayle hit his audience with a series of unsettling rhetori-cal questions: "Does America really need seventy percent of the world's lawyers? Is it healthy for our economy to have eighteen million new lawsuits coursing through the system annually?"

Then, he concluded by tying his criticisms to a significant anniversary:

On this bicentennial of the Bill of Rights, we should remind our-selves of the memorable words of Justice Robert Jackson:

"Civil liberties had their origin, and must find their ultimate guar-anty, in the faith of the people."

Our job in government, and your job as leaders in the law, is to strengthen the faith of the people—in the resolute protection of their rights, and in the effective delivery of justice.

Praise Your Audience's Role in History

When James Baker III, U.S. Secretary of State, spoke to the Aspen Institute in Berlin, Germany, he concluded his remarks on Euro-Atlantic relations this way:

> A half century ago, it would have seemed impossible that an American Secretary of State would stand in Berlin, speaking to Germans and Americans, about the values of the Euro-Atlantic community. Particularly, that he would describe ideas about securing these values in the new market democracies of Central and Eastern Europe, extending them to a Soviet Union in the throes of reform, and indeed promoting these values in the world at large.
>
> But, our predecessors have made the impossible, possible. Now it is the turn of our generation to draw out and then help sustain the Enlightenment spirit.
>
> It is most fitting that in Berlin, Freedom's City, we would chart this course.

Look at the Big Picture

On a tour of Eastern European cities, President Bush gave a particularly eloquent and well-received speech at the Karl Marx University of Economics in Budapest. He concluded with this exhortation:

"Let us have history write of us that we were the generation that made Europe whole and free."

Tell a Humorous Story to Illustrate Your Point

When Mitchell Daniels, Jr., vice president of corporate affairs for Eli Lilly, spoke at a University of Indianapolis commencement, he sent out the graduates chuckling over this bit of humor:

I will close with a story, and with sincere congratulations. . . .

The story is a favorite of President Reagan's, and concerns the businessman who ordered a floral bouquet sent to the grand opening of a friend's new branch office. He arrived at the ceremony and found to his dismay that his flowers had been delivered with a card that said, "Rest in Peace."

The next day, he called the florist and irately demanded a refund, only to be told, "Don't worry, just think of it this way. Somewhere in town yesterday some poor soul was buried under a sign that said, "Good luck in your new location."

That's what I wish you now . . . good luck in all your new locations.

Create a Memorable Scene

When Richard Armstrong, author and political consultant, spoke at the Great Lakes Cable Expo, he wrapped up his speech with this well-written, powerful summation:

Politics has always been a crazy business. Funny hats. Noisemakers. Balloons. But at least in the past, we were always looking into each other's faces. Shaking hands. Kissing babies. Arguing. Most important, compromising.

Nowadays, I'm afraid the level of our political dialogue is roughly equivalent to staring at the bathroom mirror and lip-synching to the radio.

I sincerely hope that one day soon we won't look into our cable TVs and say, "I have seen Big Brother . . . and he is me."

End with a Strong Rhetorical Question

Something like this can be effective:

"Can we afford to do it? A more relevant question is, can we afford *not* to?"

End with Words That *Sound* Strong

- "We need to return to that old-fashioned notion of competition—where *substance*, not *subsidies*, determines the winner." This ending focuses the audience's attention on two contrasting words that begin with the same syllable—*sub*.

- "We worked hard to get this department in tip-top shape. We plan to keep it that way." *Tip-top* repeats the opening and closing consonant sounds.

- "Yes, we ran into some problems. But we corrected them. Perhaps our message should be 'Sighted sub, sank same.' " Good use of alliteration—repetition of initial consonant sounds.

- "Our personnel department's training program works on the premise that 'earning' naturally follows 'learning.' " Rhyme can be catchy, but use it judiciously.

How to Make It Simple

✳ ────────────────────────────────

Speak properly, and in as few Words as you can, but
always *plainly;* for the End of Speech is not Ostentation,
but to be understood.
—William Penn

HOW TO MAKE EVERY WORD COUNT

Speeches are meant to be heard, not read. That means you
have to keep your language simple and easily understood.
Write for the ear, not the eye.

Remember: Your audience will have only one shot to
get your message. They can't go back and reread a section
that's fuzzy, as they can with a book or a newspaper article.
Get rid of any fuzzy parts *before* you give the speech.

Never be content with your first draft. *Never.* After
you've written it, read it aloud.

Let some time elapse between your rewrites. Let the
whole thing sit overnight or over a couple of nights, if possible.
Then go at it with a red pen. Cut ruthlessly. Simplify your
language.

This chapter will show you—in step-by-step detail—how
to simplify the language in your speech. It will help you:

- choose the right word

- simplify your phrases

- sharpen your sentences

Use Simple, Direct Words

Use the following list to make your own substitutions:

Instead of	*Try using*
abbreviate	shorten
accommodate	serve
advise	tell
aggregate	total, whole
anticipate	expect
approximately	about
ascertain	find out, figure out
burgeoning	growing
cessation	end
cognizant	aware
commencement	start, beginning
compel	make
component	part
conjecture	guess
currently	now
deceased	dead
demonstrate	show
desire	want
determine	find out
diminutive	little
discourse	talk
disseminate	spread
duplicate	copy
eliminate	cut out
elucidate	clarify

encounter	meet
endeavor	try
engage	hire
eradicate	wipe out
execute	do
expedite	speed
expire	die
facilitate	make easy
feasible	possible
forward	send
generate	make, cause
heretofore	until now
illustrate	show
indicate	say
initial	first
inquire	ask
locate	find
maintenance	upkeep
marginal	small
numerous	many
observe	see, watch
obtain	get
operate	work, use
originated	began
peruse	read
precipitate	cause
presently	soon
procure	get, take
recapitulate	sum up
recess	break
render	give, send
remunerate	pay
represents	is
require	need
reside	live
residence	home
retain	keep

review	check
saturate	soak
solicit	ask
stated	said
stringent	strict
submit	send
subsequent	next
substantial	large
sufficient	enough
supply	send
terminate	end
utilize	use
vacate	leave
vehicle	truck, car, van, bus
verification	proof

A final point: The Gettysburg Address is one of the world's most memorable speeches. Lincoln wrote 76 percent of it with words of *five letters or less.* Consider that an inspiration for you to do the same.

Avoid Jargon

Jargon doesn't work in a speech. It smacks of "bureaucratese" and audiences tend to block it out. It may even alienate some listeners. Get rid of it.

Jargon	*Plain English*
conceptualize	imagine
finalize	finish, complete
a guesstimate	a rough estimate
impact (verb)	affect
implement	carry out
infrastructure	foundation, framework
interface (verb)	talk with

meaningful	real
operational	okay, working
optimum	best
output	results
parameters	limits
utilization	use
viable	workable

Avoid Euphemisms

Euphemisms "bloat" a speech. Replace them with plain English.

Euphemism	Plain English
classification device	test
disadvantaged	poor
interrelated collectivity	group
inventory shrinkage	theft
motivational deprivation	laziness
negative patient care outcome	death
nomenclature	name
passed away	died
terminated	fired
unlawful or arbitrary deprivation of life	murder
unscheduled intensified repairs	emergency repairs

Avoid Vague Modifiers

Words such as "very," "slightly," and "extremely" are too vague to be useful. Use words or phrases that say *precisely* what you mean.

Vague	*Specific*
The personnel department is rather understaffed, but the situation will be corrected in the very near future.	The personnel department now has three vacancies. We will fill these jobs within the next month.

Don't Speak in Abbreviations

You may know what HEW, SEC, and FCC stand for, but don't assume that everyone else does.

You have to explain every abbreviation you use—not *every* time you use it, but at least the *first* time.

The same goes with acronyms, such as NOW for the National Organization for Women and PAC for political action committee. Unlike those abbreviations that are pronounced letter by letter (HEW, SEC, FCC, for example), acronyms are pronounced like words. You can use them in a speech, but be sure to identify them the first time.

Don't Speak in Unfamiliar Languages

If you're an English-speaking native addressing an English-speaking audience, why would you want to throw in foreign phrases? To show the audience how educated you are? To impress them with your sophistication? To display a bit of class?

Forget it.

Not everyone in your audience will know the meaning of *pro bono publico, Wanderjahr,* or *chateaux en Espagne.* For that matter, you may not even know how to pronounce them properly, and that will make you appear foolish to the more knowledgeable members of your audience.

If you want to use a foreign proverb to illustrate a point, translate it into English. For example: "The French have a wonderful saying, 'The more things change, the more they stay the same.' This sentiment certainly describes our organization. We've served this community for fifty years. We've changed our structure along the way, but we haven't changed our goals."

On the other hand, *if you were born or reared in a foreign country,* you may use your native language to great effect.

Find an appropriate proverb from your native country . . . work it into your speech . . . offer it to the audience in your native tongue . . . pause . . . then give the English translation.

This well-timed delivery can greatly increase audience interest and help build emotional appeal.

When Jeffrey Steiner, chairman and CEO of the Fairchild Corporation, spoke on the 500th anniversary of the arrival of Jews in Turkey, he included a Yiddish proverb:

In 1942, when Sephardic Jews were expelled from Spain, they found a safe haven in Turkey. And, for half a millennium, Turkey has continued to extend a special benevolence to Jewish people fleeing persecution.

I know. I was one of those people. During World War II, my family sought refuge in Turkey. We were able to escape the Nazis, and flee Vienna, and find safety in Istanbul. . . .

The history of the Jewish community in Turkey is remarkable. There is a Yiddish proverb that fits the spirit of our shared history: "Mountains cannot meet, but men can."

You see, for half a millennium, the republic of Turkey has proven that men and women of good will *can* meet . . . that tolerance and respect *can* cross the "mountains" of geographic borders . . . that people of different faiths *can* live together in harmony.

Avoid Sexist Language

There are several ways to avoid sexist implications in your speech.

Find substitutes for compound nouns that contain man or woman. This list should help:

businessmen	business people
cleaning woman	office cleaner
Congressmen	members of Congress
firemen	fire fighters
foreman	supervisor
housewife	homemaker
insurance salesman	insurance agent
mailmen	mail carriers
man-hours	worker-hours
man's achievements	human achievements
mankind	human beings
manpower	labor force
policeman	police officer
political man	political behavior
repairman	repairperson/service rep
salesmen	sales reps, sales clerks, sales force
spokesman	spokesperson
statesman	leader
stewardess	flight attendant

Shift to the plural

Before	*After*
When a *manager* goes on a business trip, *he* should save all of *his* receipts.	When *managers* go on business trips, *they* should save all of *their* receipts.
A utility tax hits the *consumer* where *he* is already overburdened.	A utility tax hits *consumers* where *they* are already overburdened.

Restructure the sentence

Before	After
The company will select someone from the Treasury Department *to be chairman* of the Travel and Entertainment Committee.	The company will select someone from the Treasury Department *to head* the Travel and Entertainment Committee.

Alternate male and female examples

Before	After
Interviewers are too quick to say, *"He* doesn't have enough technical knowledge," or *"He's* just not the right *man* for us."	Interviewers are too quick to say, *"He* doesn't have enough technical knowledge," or *"She's* just not the right *person* for us."

Be sure that you don't always mention the male first. Switch the order: husbands and wives, hers or his, him or her, women and men.

Avoid male/female stereotypes

Doctors, nurses, and even astronauts come in both sexes. Do *not* refer to someone as a "female doctor" or a "male nurse." It's gratuitous.

SIMPLIFY YOUR PHRASES

> Everything should be made as simple as possible, but not simpler.
> —Albert Einstein

A phrase with too many words becomes meaningless.

Look at your draft, and get rid of pompous, wordy, and overwritten constructions. Use the following list as a guideline:

Instead of	*Try using*
a large number of	many
a sufficient number of	enough
a total of 42	42
advance planning	planning
are in agreement with	agree
as indicated in the following chart	the following chart shows
as you know	*Delete* (If they already know, why tell them?)
at that point in time	then
at the present time	now
at the time of presenting this speech	today
basically unaware of	did not know
be that as it may	but
blame it on	blame
both alike	alike
brief in duration	short
bring the matter to the attention of	tell
caused damage to	damaged
check into the facts	check the facts
consensus of opinion	consensus
continue on	continue
curiously enough	curiously
demonstrate the ability to	can
despite the fact that	although
due to the fact that	because
end product	product
equally as	equally
estimated at about	estimated at
exert a leadership role	lead
firm commitment	commitment
for free	free
for the purpose of	for

frame of reference	viewpoint, perspective
give encouragement to	encourage
have a discussion	discuss
hold a meeting	meet
hold in abeyance	suspend
in the majority of instances	most often, usually
in the area of	approximately
in connection with	on, of
in close proximity	near
in view of	because
in the event of	if
in the vicinity of	near
in order to	to
in many cases	often
in some cases	sometimes
in the course of	during
individuals who will participate	participants
is of the opinion that	thinks
is in an operational state	operates, works
is equipped with	has
is noted to have	has
it is recognized that	*Delete*
it is recommended by me that	I recommend
it has been shown that	*Delete*
it may be mentioned that	*Delete*
join together	join (unless in a marriage ceremony, where "join together" is acceptable)
made a complete reversal	reversed
make a decision	decide
my personal opinion	my opinion
needless to say	*Delete* (If you don't *need* to say it, why *would* you say it?)
new innovations	innovations

newly created	new
never before in the past	never
obtain an estimate of	estimate
of sufficient magnitude	big enough
off of	off
on a national basis	nationally
on the basis of	from
on the occasion of	when
optimum utilization	best use
over with	over
past experience	experience
personal friend	friend
predicated on	based on
prior to	before
provide assistance to	help
start off	start
study in depth	study
subsequent to	after
take action	act
the major portion	most
the reason why is that	because
until such time as	until
very unique	unique
was in communication with	talked with
with reference to	about
with the result that	so that
with regard to	about
with the exception of	except
would invoke an expenditure of approximately	would cost about

AVOID THE FLUFF PITFALL

If your speech is filled with statements such as "This has been a most challenging year," or "We all face a golden opportunity," or "We will meet our challenges with optimism and view the future with confidence," it is probably high on fluff and low on content. Unfortunately, too many business speeches fall into this category.

To get rid of fluff, try this experiment. Listen to ten ordinary business speeches and count the number of times words such as "challenge" and "opportunity" are used. Pay careful attention to the opening and closing sections of the speeches, because that's where amateur writers tend to throw in the most fluff.

Then, listen to ten speeches that you can assume to be "ghostwritten"—speeches, for example, that are given by the President of the United States. These speeches will have fewer "challenges" and "opportunities" in their texts. Why? Because professional speechwriters try to avoid such fluff. They know that audiences block it out.

Follow the professionals. Review your speech and get rid of any glib expressions. If you want your message to stand out, put content—not fluff—into your speech.

SHARPEN YOUR SENTENCES

> When "whom" is correct, use some other formulation.
> —William Safire

There are several important things to know about sentences.

Short sentences are stronger than long sentences

Try this experiment: Take a sample page from your draft and count the number of words in each sentence. Write the numbers down and average them.

If you average twenty or more words per sentence, you'd better start cutting. Why? Because an audience can't follow what you're saying if you put too many words in a sentence. Your message just gets lost.

If you don't believe me, read your longest sentence aloud,

then read your shortest sentence aloud. See which one is more powerful—and more memorable.

Variety is the spice of life

If all your sentences are long, no one will be able to follow you. But if all your sentences are short, your speech may become boring. People get tired of hearing the same rhythm. If you use a rather long sentence, precede or follow it with a short, punchy one. The contrast will catch your audience's attention.

FDR was a master of this technique, and his speeches show a great sense of rhythm and timing. Consider the following example. He uses a powerful, two-word sentence followed by a rhythmic, eighteen-word sentence:

> Hostilities exist. There is no mincing the fact that our people, our territory and our interests are in grave danger.

Ronald Reagan also knew how to vary the rhythm of his speech:

> Everyone is against protectionism in the abstract. That is easy. It is another matter to make the hard, courageous choices when it is your industry or your business that appears to be hurt by foreign competition. I know. We in the United States deal with the problem of protectionism every day of the year.

Count the words he used: seven in the first sentence, then three, then twenty-six, then two, then sixteen. Average length? About eleven words per sentence.

Use the active, not the passive, voice

It's time for a grammar lesson. I'll keep it brief.

These sentences are in the *active voice* because they show that the subject acts, or does something:

> The Customer Inquiry Department *answers* almost four hundred phone calls every day.

Our new maintenance program *saved* the company $5,000 in the first six months.

The committee *records* all suggestions in a log book.

Government *must place* some constraints on these contracts to prevent price excesses.

A sentence is in the *passive voice* when the subject is acted upon:

- Almost four hundred phone calls *are answered* by the Customer Inquiry Department every day.

- $5,000 *was saved* by the company in the first six months of our new maintenance program.

- All suggestions *are recorded* by the committee in a log book.

- Some constraints *must be placed* on these contracts by government to prevent price excesses.

Read the above sentences aloud, and notice that the active voice:

1. sounds more vigorous

2. is more personal

3. uses fewer words

4. is easier to follow

5. is easier to remember

Get rid of passive constructions in your speech. They sound stilted, flat, and contrived.

Cut "I think," "I believe," "I know," "It seems to me that," "In my opinion"

These expressions weaken sentences. Cut them, and you will make your sentences stronger.

Before	*After*
We think prices are already too high and we know people are hurting.	Prices are already too high and people are hurting.

Avoid "There are"

Sentences that begin with "There are . . ." are often weak. Try rewriting them.

Before	*After*
There are alternative ways that must be found by us to solve the problem.	We must find other ways to solve the problem.

Beware of tongue twisters

Read your speech aloud several times, and listen carefully for potential tongue twisters.

Try to round up a couple of junior high youngsters and have them listen to your speech. They are notorious for spotting potential tongue twisters, especially those that sound obscene. Better to have some junior high kids spot an embarrassing phrase than to have your audience laugh at it.

A QUICK SUMMATION

A final bit of advice from George Orwell on how to make your writing simple:

1. Never use a long word where a short one will do.

2. If it is possible to cut out a word, always cut it out.

3. Never use the passive where you can use the active.

4. Never use a foreign phrase, a scientific word, or a jargon word if you can think of an everyday English equivalent.

5. Break any of these rules sooner than say anything barbarous.

Style

Whatever you do, kid, always serve it with a little
dressing.
—George M. Cohan (advice to Spencer Tracy)

Business executives, politicians, and civic leaders give thousands of speeches every day. Most of these speeches are forgotten as soon as the audience leaves the room—if not sooner.

But, some speeches *do* linger in the minds and hearts of
audiences. What makes these speeches special? Style.

Speeches with style have a certain "ring" that makes them
easy to remember. They have a psychological appeal that
makes them seem *important* to remember. And they create an
impact that makes them irresistibly *quotable*.

Here are some techniques that professional speechwriters
use.

HOW TO USE TRIPARTITE DIVISION

Tripartite division is a device that breaks things into three
parts. Three has always been a powerful number. Consider:

- the Holy Trinity
- the three wise men and their three gifts
- God's three attributes: omniscience, omnipotence, and omnipresence
- Goldilocks and the three bears
- the scientific method: hypothesis, inference, and verification
- in baseball: Three strikes and you're out!
- from the battlefield: Ready! Aim! Fire!

For some mysterious reason, the human mind is strongly attracted to things that come in "three's." You can make this attraction work for you by using tripartite division in speeches. Throughout history, speakers have known that tripartite division is a powerful mnemonic device.

- *Julius Caesar:* "Veni, vidi, vici." ("I came, I saw, I conquered.")
- *Abraham Lincoln:* "We cannot dedicate, we cannot consecrate, we cannot hallow this ground."
- *Franklin Delano Roosevelt:* "I see one-third of a nation ill-housed, ill-clad, ill-nourished."
- *Ronald Reagan:* "We will never compromise our principles and standards. We will never give away our freedom. We will never abandon our belief in God."

Admittedly these are some of the biggest names of history. But we ordinary people can make tripartite division work to our advantage, too.

- *a department manager:* "We need to develop guidelines, establish controls, and set limits."

- *a civic leader:* "The promise is there, the logic is over-whelming, the need is great."

- *the recipient of an award for community service:* "My volunteer work has been my life, my inspiration, my joy."

- *a bank manager:* "We do not wield the power we once did—power over our employees, our customers, our communities."

HOW TO USE PARALLELISM

Use a parallel structure to create balance—the emotional appeal of harmony.

- *John Fitzgerald Kennedy:* "If a free society cannot help the many who are poor, it cannot save the few who are rich."

- *Richard Nixon:* "Where peace is unknown, make it welcome; where peace is fragile, make it strong; where peace is temporary, make it permanent."

- *St. Francis of Assisi:* "Lord, make me an instrument of Your peace; where there is hatred, let me sow love; where there is injury, pardon; where there is discord, union; where there is doubt, faith; where there is despair, hope; where there is darkness, light; and where there is sadness, joy."

- *a steel executive:* "We must analyze the problem, then we must find the solution."

- *an honoree:* "And, as we rediscover our priorities, let us rediscover our humanity."

- *a college president:* "We expect to be around for a long time, and we expect to remain strong for a long time."

HOW TO USE IMAGERY

Be specific, be vivid, be colorful . . . and you will make your point. Even better, your audience will *remember* your point.

- *Winston Churchill:* "An iron curtain has descended across the continent."

- *Franklin Delano Roosevelt:* "When you see a rattlesnake poised to strike, you do not wait until he has struck before you crush him."

- *Lech Walesa:* "By no means do I want to topple the government; I just want to stick a pin in its backside so that it picks up the pace a little bit."

- *Drug czar William Bennett:* "If you don't get tough on drugs, they will get tough on you."

HOW TO USE INVERSION OF ELEMENTS

If you switch the elements in paired statements, you can produce some memorable lines.

- *John Fitzgerald Kennedy:* "Ask not what your country can do for you. Ask what you can do for your country."

- *a store owner:* "We would rather be a big fish in a small pond than a small fish in a big pond."

HOW TO USE REPETITION

Audiences do not always pay attention. Their minds wander. They think about the work that's piled up on their desks. They think about the bills that are piled up at home. They often miss whole sections of a speech.

If you have an important word or phrase or sentence, be sure to repeat it. Again. And again. Jesse Jackson knew how to use this technique in his campaign speeches for the presidential nomination: "We must give peace a chance. We must give peace a chance. We must, we must!"

When H. Norman Schwarzkopf, hero of Operation Desert Storm, returned to the U.S. to deliver an address before the Joint Session of Congress, he used repetition to drive home a point with enormous power and pride:

> We were all volunteers and we were regulars. We were Reservists and we were National Guardsmen, serving side by side as we have in every war, because that's what the U.S. military is.
>
> And, we were men and women, each of us bearing our fair share of the load and none of us quitting because the conditions were too rough or the job was too tough, because that's what your military is.
>
> We were Protestants and Catholics and Jews and Moslems and Buddhists and many other religions fighting for a common and just cause, because that's what your military is.
>
> We were black and white and yellow and brown and red, and we noticed when our blood was shed in the desert it didn't separate by race but it flowed together, because that's what your military is. . . .
>
> We left our homes and our families and traveled thousands of miles away and fought in places whose names we couldn't even pronounce simply because you asked us to and it therefore became our duty, because that's what your military does.

Finally, listen to this use of repetition by South African leader Nelson Mandela:

> Apartheid must go, and it must go now. The masses of the American people are with us. Both [the House] and the Senate of the United States are with us. President Bush and the administration are with us. Surely, apartheid will go.

HOW TO USE RHETORICAL QUESTIONS

How to Ask rhetorical questions to *involve* your audience. Pause a moment or so after each question. This will allow listeners some time to answer the question in their own minds—and it will help reinforce your message.

- *Robert Clarke, Comptroller of the Currency:* "Remember when people used to say: 'It's as safe as money in the bank?' Remember when people used to say: 'It's as solid as the bank on the corner?' "

- *Grammy-winning singer, k.d. lang* (on behalf of animal rights): "We all love animals, but why do we call some of them pets and some of them dinner?"

- *Lee Iacocca:* "How are we going to compete in a high-technology world when we are turning out students who can't figure percentages and don't know what gravity is?"

- *Comedian Jay Leno:* "Iraq attacks Kuwait, there's an upheaval in Liberia, there's an attempted coup in the Philippines. . . . You ever get the feeling that the Goodwill Games just didn't work out this year?"

EIGHT

Humor: What Works, What Doesn't, and Why

If you want to rule the world, you must keep it amused.
—Ralph Waldo Emerson

Some people think they absolutely must use a joke to begin a speech. I hope you are not one of these people.

Jokes can be risky. There's nothing worse than a joke that falls flat—unless it's a joke that falls flat at the beginning of a speech. Beware.

Ask yourself five questions before you plan to use a joke *anywhere* in your speech:

- "Will this joke tie into the subject and mood of my speech?"

- "Will my audience feel comfortable with this joke?"

- "Is the joke short and uncomplicated?"

- "Is the joke fresh?"

- "Can I deliver this joke really well—with confidence and ease and perfect timing?"

If you can't answer "yes" to all of these questions, scrap the joke.

USE A LIGHT TOUCH

Professional comedians like jokes that produce loud laughs. But you are a speaker, not a professional comedian.

Don't focus on jokes that beg for loud laughs because this usually backfires. Instead, try to develop a "light touch" of humor. You can do this through:

- personal anecdotes
- one-liners that blend into the speech
- humorous quotations
- quips that seem off-the-cuff (but are actually planned)
- clever statistics
- careful choice of words
- gestures
- voice intonations
- raising an eyebrow
- smiling

Using a light touch of humor will help the audience to see you as a decent, humane, friendly person. It will help put the audience in a receptive mood for the message of your speech.

WHAT WORKS

What kind of humor works best in a speech? The kind that is friendly and personal and natural. Humor in a speech doesn't need to produce guffaws. A few smiles and some chuckles are just fine for your purpose.

Where can you find this humor? Many speakers buy

books of jokes and adapt the material to suit their own needs. These sources can be helpful, but *only* if you use them judiciously. *Don't* use the material verbatim. Always adapt the humor to your own needs and your own style.

Learn to create *your own* light touches of humor. Original material will work better than material that is lifted straight from books.

Why? Three big reasons:

1. If you create your own humorous touches, you can be sure this material will be fresh to your audience.

2. If the humor comes from your own experience, you will deliver it more naturally and more effectively.

3. If you share something personal with the audience, they will feel more friendly toward you.

Your safest bet for good humor in a speech is to poke gentle fun at yourself. Try making light of:

- *Your fame.* A little boy once asked John F. Kennedy how he became a war hero. "It was absolutely involuntary," Kennedy replied. "They sank my boat."

- *Your image.* When Barbara Bush appeared in front of more than six thousand people at a "Salute to the First Lady," she won cheers with this bit of humor about her down-to-earth image:

  "Speaking of glamour, I want you to look at me very carefully." Pointing to herself all dressed up, she said, "Please notice the hair, the makeup, designer clothes . . . I want you to watch me all week and remember—You may never see it again."

- *Your problems.* Retired Lt. Col. Oliver North said at the start of his speech at the Pennsylvania Fair, "It's nice to be invited somewhere without a subpoena."

- *Your own company.* Mimi Feller, vice president of public affairs for Gannett (which publishes *USA Today*), teased her own company when she addressed the Omaha Press Club:

There was a joke going around for a while. How would the USA's major newspapers headline the ultimate news story, the end of the world?

The *New York Times:* "World Ends; Third World Countries Hardest Hit";

The *Washington Post:* "World Ends; Reagan Says He Can't Remember It Happening";

The Wall Street Journal: "World Ends; Stock Market Halts Trading Early";

The *Omaha World-Herald:* "World Ends; Mike Boyle Finally Throws in the Towel";

USA Today: "We're Gone! State-by-State Demise, Page 5A; Final *Final* Sports Results, Page 6C."

That's *USA Today*—upbeat and to the point.

- *The weaknesses of your organization.* Listen to the way Kathleen Shields, supervisor of the Immigration Naturalization Service's information unit, described the slow progress of her organization:

"We're slowly but surely moving into the twentieth century, but by the time we get there, it will be the twenty-first."

- *Your success.* When Eugene Antonio Marino was named the first black Catholic archbishop in the U.S., he told a self-deprecating joke to his Atlanta supporters:

This may have come about through misdirected prayer. Some people were praying for a new archbishop, and some were praying even more fervently for a strong backup quarterback for the Falcons. Somebody up there sent in the wrong Marino. Instead of Dan from the Miami Dolphins, they got Eugene from the D.C. diocese.

- *The way the audience perceives your company.* When Harold Carr, vice president of public relations for the Boeing Company, spoke to a meeting of public relations people, he created a sense of rapport with this bit of self-deprecating humor:

> I must say I was a little surprised when Bill James asked me to talk with you on crisis communications. I am aware, after all, of the occasional journalist's complaint that Boeing won't discuss even the simplest issues during the calmest of times. To which I can only respond "no comment." . . .
>
> There's even the claim that we take our guidance on press relations from that great communicator, President Calvin Coolidge, who was reliably reported to have conducted a press conference that went something like this:
>
> "Do you have any comment about tariffs, Mr. President?"
>
> "No."
>
> "Do you have any comment on the farm bill?"
>
> "No."
>
> "Mr. President, do you have any comment on the naval appropriation?"
>
> "No."
>
> Then, as the reporters were leaving to write up their notes, Coolidge shouted to them, "And don't quote me!"

A Caution

Poking fun at yourself is the safest kind of humor, but never belittle your professional competence in your area of expertise. Otherwise, the audience will wonder why they should bother listening to you.

And never say anything about yourself that you might regret later. A speech is over in fifteen or twenty minutes, but a reputation lasts a lifetime. Don't sacrifice a reputation for a cheap laugh.

OTHER AREAS FOR HUMOR

You can generally make fun of big government, politicians, and high taxes with complete impunity. Audiences *like* to hear speakers make fun of these things; indeed, they often look forward to these digs.

Of course, you can always get some good mileage out of the weather. Consider this example from David Rockefeller, chairman of Chase Manhattan Bank:

> Coming to Southern California is a delightful way to begin the spring, although your kind invitation might have been even more welcome in the dead of winter. At that time, however, I understand this area was being hit by floods, mud slides, and earth tremors. Somebody probably figured that the last thing you needed was a great gust of wind from the East. I will try to spare you that calamity this afternoon.

WHAT ARE YOUR CHANCES OF GETTING A LAUGH?

You'll find it's easier to get a laugh as the day goes on. Why? Because it's usually easier to get *anything* as the day goes on.

Think about it:

Early in the morning, people are still groggy. Their minds often aren't working well. If they think about anything at all, they think about the pile of work that lies ahead of them. They just want to have a cup of coffee and get moving with their schedule. They're not in a very playful mood—and it's hard to be funny when the audience doesn't want to play along.

So, if you're the guest speaker at a breakfast fund-raiser, for example, keep everything short and simple. Even if the audience is really interested in your cause, they will be anxious to get out of the meeting and get on with the day's work. No complicated jokes, please. A quick one-liner is probably all these people can handle.

By lunchtime, things ease up a bit. At least some of the day's work is done, and people can sit back and relax a little. But, still, they have to get back to the office, and they will be looking at their watches as two o'clock approaches.

By dinnertime, things are as loose as they'll ever be. Work is over. People want to put their troubles behind them for a while. They're in the mood to unwind. Indulge them. Give them the chuckles they *want.*

By late evening, however, things may be *too* loose for humor to work. In fact, things may be too loose for *anything* to work . . . including the speaker! By ten or eleven o'clock, most audiences are either too inattentive, too inebriated, or too tired to be receptive to any message.

At this late hour, you must put aside your ego and put aside your prepared speech—no matter how witty or wise that speech might be.

Just give a three-or-four sentence capsule summary, flash a broad smile, and get out of there. The audience will love you for it.

WHAT ABOUT DELIVERY?

A good delivery will greatly increase your chances of getting a good laugh.

You must be in complete control of the joke or anecdote. You must understand every word, every pause, every nuance. You must—above all—have a good sense of timing.

Want to see how important good delivery is? Practice this fifth-century line from Saint Augustine: "Give me chastity and continence, but not just now." The pause after "continence" makes the whole line.

Don't set yourself up for failure by announcing, "Here's

a really funny story." Let the audience decide for themselves if it's really funny or not.

And be prepared in case the audience thinks it *isn't* funny. The only thing worse than the silence that follows a failed joke is the sound of the speaker laughing while the audience sits in embarrassed silence. Don't laugh at your own jokes. As Archie Bunker used to say to Edith, "Stifle yourself."

A FEW WORDS ABOUT SWEARING

Swearing can work in a speech—*if* you know your audience and *if* you choose your words carefully.

When David Brinkley spoke at the annual Chicago Communications luncheon, he included this story about former Vice President Spiro Agnew:

> If I were to go on the air tomorrow night and say "Spiro Agnew is the greatest American statesman since Adams, Hamilton, Jefferson, Washington," the audience would think I'd gone crazy. But Agnew wouldn't. He'd say, "The son of a bitch has finally come to his senses."

David Brinkley knew how to make a point. And you can bet the audience remembered his story.

Just one word about dirty jokes, racial jokes, ethnic jokes, ageist jokes, and sexist jokes:

The word is: *don't.*

Don't use them, *ever.*

These jokes have no place in a business or political speech. If you use them, they will come back to haunt you.

Remember the time Jesse Jackson referred to New York City as "Hymietown." Comments like this are not forgotten.

NINE

Special-Occasion Speeches

Words are what hold society together.
—Stuart Chase

Not all speeches deal with big issues. Many speeches are simply ceremonial. They honor a person's retirement, or present an award, or dedicate a new building.

These speeches are different from the standard public speech. They're usually much shorter, and they often take a personal approach.

This chapter will give some guidelines on:

- the invocation
- the commencement speech
- the award or tribute speech

It will also help you with some specialized speaking skills:

- how to introduce a speaker
- how to give an impromptu speech
- how to organize a panel presentation
- how to handle a question-and-answer session

THE INVOCATION

> The fewer words, the better prayer.
> —Martin Luther

The scene: You're sitting on a dais at a banquet. The evening's event? To honor a local business executive with a humanitarian award.

Just before the banquet begins, the master of ceremonies learns that the clergyman who was supposed to offer the invocation can't attend. They need someone to fill in, and they turn to you. "Would you be kind enough to offer grace?"

Well, *would* you? Even more to the point, *could* you?

Could you come up with an invocation that's appropriate for a mixed business gathering—a gathering that might include Catholics, Jews, Protestants, and others?

Avoid prayers that represent a specific religious preference.

A decidedly Protestant prayer, for example, might exclude some parts of the audience. What's worse, it might even *offend* some parts of the audience. I am reminded of an unfortunate invocation that ended with, "We pray for this in Jesus' name." Well, the Jewish man sitting next to me certainly wasn't praying in Jesus' name—and he resented the arrogance of the person who gave that prayer.

Don't give an invocation that might alienate some people in your audience. Instead, come up with something that shows respect for all people—something that honors human dignity.

In a business setting, it's appropriate to:

- give thanks for all blessings

- pray for peace

- ask for wisdom and courage and strength to deal with your problems

Above all, keep it short—under a minute, if you can.

A word of caution about humorous invocations: *don't.* This is not the time to use a light touch. Avoid *anything* such as "Good food, good meat, good God, let's eat." (Yes, I'm told someone actually used that invocation at a civic organization.)

THE COMMENCEMENT SPEECH

> Proclaim not all thou knowest.
> —Benjamin Franklin

Everyone is in a good mood at a commencement. Students are glad to be finished with exams. Parents are glad to be finished with tuition bills. And instructors are glad to be finished with another academic year.

Don't let long-winded or pompous remarks put them in a bad mood.

Remember: Caps and gowns can be hot. Folding chairs can be uncomfortable. Crowded gymnasiums can be unbearably stuffy. Follow Franklin Delano Roosevelt's advice: "Be brief . . . be sincere . . . be seated."

In the process, of course, try to say something inspirational, thoughtful, encouraging, uplifting, or memorable. The Academy Award–winning actress Meryl Streep knew this when she returned to speak at her alma mater, Vassar College. She encouraged the graduates to strive for excellence, even though life might be difficult at times. "If you can live with the devil," Streep said, "then Vassar has not sunk its teeth into you." This proved to be a great line for a commencement speech—easy for the audience to remember, and irresistible for the press to quote.

It's safest to speak for between ten and fifteen minutes. If you go on longer, the audience may get dangerously restless. After all, a graduating class doesn't have to worry anymore about reprisals from the school principal or the college president. They're free to yawn or talk or even boo. Don't make any remarks about the brevity (or verbosity) of your speech. I once heard a commencement speaker promise to be brief. He was, much to his embarrassment, applauded by a few rambunctious students.

Remember that June weather is notoriously fickle. If the commencement is outdoors, be alert to the storm clouds and be prepared to shorten your address if the rains come.

Also, make sure your hat's on tight. More than one commencement speaker has been embarrassed by a hat flying off into the wind.

PRESENTING AN AWARD

> 'Tis an old maxim in the schools,
> That flattery's the food of fools;
> Yet now and then your men of wit
> Will condescend to take a bit.
> —Jonathan Swift

A person who retires after forty years of service. An employee who contributes a money-saving idea to the company. A telephone installer who saves a customer's life. All of these people deserve some special recognition, and you may be asked to give a speech in honor of one of them.

These five guidelines should help:

1. *Be generous with the praise.* If one of your employees risked his life to save a customer's life and he's now receiving a special award, you must come up with praise to match the occasion. Be generous.

2. *Be specific.* Whatever you say should be so specific that it couldn't possibly be said about anyone else. Never, *never* give an award speech that sounds "canned."

   For example, if the person is retiring after forty

years with the company, mention two or three specific projects he was involved in. Tell how his involvement made a difference.

3. *Be personal.* Make your tribute reveal a flesh-and-blood person. Show the honoree's personality and vulnerability.

   One good way to personalize your presentation: Ask the honoree's friends and family for some special recollections. Include a few of these "real-life" stories when you make your presentation.

4. *Be sincere.* Suppose you must give an award to a person you've never met. Don't pretend to be a close friend or associate. Simply get some information about the person from a supervisor and share this information in a sincere, straightforward way.

   For example, "Karen's supervisor has told me how Karen saved a baby's life. I'm glad to meet Karen and to present her with this award for distinguished service. I'm proud to have her as one of our employees."

5. *Be inspirational.* The Reverend Peter Gomes said this in a memorial tribute to Martin Luther King, Jr., at Harvard University: "We remember Martin Luther King, Jr., not because of his success, but because of our failures; not because of the work he has done, but because of the work we must do."

INTRODUCING A SPEAKER

Your assignment is to introduce a speaker. That's simple. Just call the speaker and ask for a written introduction—not a resume or a vita, but a completely written introduction that you can deliver.

What a Good Introduction Should Include

A good introduction should be brief—certainly no more than four minutes, and preferably just a minute or two.

It should include:

- several mentions of the speaker's name
- the speaker's qualifications to talk about the topic
- the title of the speech

A good introduction should present this information in a friendly, personal way. It should *not* sound like a resume. It should *not* sound like a repetition of the biographical data already printed on the program.

If the speaker provides you with a stuffy introduction, rewrite it to sound friendlier. For example, delete a boring list of professional organizations and fill in with an anecdote that shows what kind of person the speaker is.

If the introduction provided is too modest, add some material that shows the speaker's unique qualifications. Quote the speaker, if possible, or quote someone else's remarks showing the speaker's special attributes.

Introduction Dos

- Be sure to pronounce the speaker's name correctly. (Verify the pronunciation in advance.)

- Repeat the speaker's name several times during the introduction so the audience can catch it.

- At the end of the introduction, face the audience (*not* the speaker) and announce the speaker's name: "We couldn't have found a more qualified hospital administrator than . . . Peggy Smith."

- Then turn to the speaker and smile.

- In formal situations, applaud until the speaker reaches your side, shake hands, and return to your place.

- In informal situations, sit down as soon as the speaker rises and starts toward the lectern.

- Pay close attention to the speaker's opening. It may contain a reference to you, and you should be prepared to smile or nod in response.

- Plan these movements carefully. Make sure the speaker knows the last line of your introduction so he or she can use it as a cue.

Introduction Don'ts

- Don't upstage the speaker by making your introduction *too* funny. (Let the speaker be the star.)

- Don't try to present a capsule summary of the speaker's speech. (You might misinterpret the speaker's focus, and that would put the speaker at a serious disadvantage.)

- Don't steal the speaker's material. (If the speaker told you a good anecdote over lunch last week, don't use it. The speaker might have planned to use it in the speech.)

- Don't rely on memory. (Write out your introduction in full.)

- Don't ad-lib. (Many a "spontaneous" comment has turned into an inane one—especially after a few drinks.)

- Don't draw attention to any negative conditions. (For example, don't say, "We're glad that Josephine has recovered from her heart attack and that she can be with us today." Comments like this do *not* put an audience in a relaxed mood.)

- Don't try to con the audience by saying things such as, "This is the funniest speaker you'll ever hear." (Let the audience make up their own minds.)

• Don't put pressure on the speaker by saying, "Now we'll see whether or not he's an excellent speaker, which I expect he is." (I once heard a CEO make such an introduction, and the speaker looked terrified.)

Seven Cliches That Never Work in an Introduction

These cliches do a disservice to you and to the poor speaker who must follow your introduction. Avoid:

1. "Ladies and gentlemen, here is a speaker who needs no introduction. . . ."
2. "We are truly honored to have with us today . . ."
3. "Without further ado . . ."
4. "It is indeed a high privilege . . ."
5. "On this most memorable and ceremonial occasion . . ."
6. "Ladies and gentlemen, heeeere's . . ."
7. "We are a lucky audience because we have none other than . . ."

I have heard all these introductions used by supposedly intelligent people. I wished I had not, and so did the rest of the audience.

A Tacky Introduction

How many times have you heard someone stand up on a banquet dais and say, "I'd like to introduce Mr. John Jones and his good wife, Nancy"?

What, exactly, is a "good" wife? If John Jones had a "bad" wife, would the host announce that, too?

Get rid of "the good wife" or "the better half." Such phrases are tacky and belittling. Just say, "I'd like to introduce John and Nancy Jones."

THE IMPROMPTU SPEECH

Mark Twain once said, "It takes three weeks to prepare a good ad-lib speech." Alas, he was right. If you're going to a meeting where someone *might* ask you to speak, gather your thoughts in advance.

Ask yourself, "What is likely to happen at this meeting? Who will be there? What will they probably say? Are there any controversial areas? Will people have questions for me? How should I respond?"

Make notes about the topics you think will come up. Practice some impromptus until you are comfortable and convincing. Be sure to practice *aloud*. Your thoughts can't count until they're spoken—and heard.

Perhaps the worst thing that can happen at a meeting is for someone to ask you for an answer/opinion/analysis, and the request catches you totally off guard. You've never given the subject a thought. You don't have any facts or figures. You're in deep trouble, right?

Not necessarily. If you have poise, your audience will forgive you almost anything. Keep your head high, your back straight, your shoulders relaxed, your eyes alert, your voice strong, your pitch moderate.

Above all, don't apologize. Never say anything like, "Oh, I'm so sorry. I feel so embarrassed. I didn't know you'd ask me to speak. I don't have any information with me."

No one expects you to give a keynote address under these circumstances. Just make a comment. If you can't come up with an intelligent response, keep your poise, maintain direct eye contact, and say, in an even voice, "I don't know. I will look into that and get back to you with the information."

How to Organize an Impromptu Speech

- Decide what you want to talk about—*fast!*

- Commit yourself to that approach. Don't change subjects or reverse your opinion midstream.

- Feel free to pause for a few seconds to collect your thoughts. The audience will not think you're stupid; they'll admire you for being able to organize your ideas under difficult circumstances.

- Open with a generalization to stall for time, if necessary. "Deregulation is certainly an important issue right now" will buy you a few extra seconds to compose your response.

- Or, repeat the question to stall for extra time. "You're asking me about the changes that deregulation will bring to the banking industry." Repeating the question has an extra benefit: It makes sure the audience knows what you've been asked to speak about.

- Present just two or three points of evidence. Do not bore the audience with chronological details.

- Wrap up your impromptu speech with a firm conclusion—a punch line that people can focus on.

- Do not ramble. Once you've offered what sounds like a conclusion, just stop.

PANEL PRESENTATIONS

How to Moderate

- Seat the panelists three or four minutes in advance—just long enough to allow them to get their papers in order.

- Make sure they have glasses of water, with extra pitchers on the table. Also make sure they have stopwatches.

- Use large name cards to identify the panelists (by first and last names).

- Start the presentation on time.

- Introduce yourself right away. I once heard a moderator, an editor, ramble on for seventeen minutes before she gave her name. The members of the audience kept whispering to each other, "Who is she? Who is she?" I'm sure they were also wondering, "What's she doing up there?"

- Make sure the audience is comfortable. If people are standing at the back of the room, tell them there are seats available at the front, then pause and allow them to move forward. If you don't take care of these logistics at the beginning, you'll be bothered by rustling noises throughout the panel presentation.

- As you introduce the panelists, use their names two or three times. Unless you are introducing J. D. Salinger, do *not* use initials. Give everyone a first name.

- Tell the purpose of the panel presentation.

- Explain *how* the panel will work (number of minutes allowed for each panelist, time for rebuttals, questions and answers, etc.).

- Give the panelists a "thirty-second signal" so they can wrap up their presentations. One effective technique: Simply show the panelist a 3 × 5 card that reads "30 seconds."

- If panelists run overtime, interrupt them—nicely, of course—and give them fifteen seconds to finish.

- *Do not* let any panelist abuse your schedule. Say in a firm, even voice, "Thank you, Mrs. Smith, but your time is up."

- Close the presentation on schedule with a few words of thanks to the panelists and to the audience.

How to Be a Panelist

- Be prepared for the worst. Inexperienced moderators may not know the above guidelines. Try to make the best of the situation.

- If the moderator forgot name cards or didn't pronounce your name properly, start by saying, "Hello. I'm *(name)*."

- If the moderator didn't give you an adequate introduction, briefly give your credentials and explain why you're there.

- If you are the last speaker and the time has run out, know how to give a shortened presentation.

- If another panelist refuses to stop speaking and the moderator can't control the situation, you may be forced to assert yourself. Take heart from Maxine Waters, the state legislator from Los Angeles. When Senator Gary Hart was trying to woo delegates to the National Women's Political Caucus convention in San Antonio, he supposedly ignored five warnings that his time was up. Maxine Waters, one of the panelists, finally demanded, "What does your refusal to relinquish the podium say about your attitude toward women?" What, indeed?

QUESTION-AND-ANSWER SESSIONS

There aren't any embarrassing questions—just embarrassing answers.

—Ambassador Carl T. Rowan, Jr.

A question-and-answer session can make or break your speech. Plan to make the Q&A work *for* you, not *against* you. You should prepare for a Q&A as carefully as you prepare for a speech. Always develop a list of possible questions. Be realistic. If you're giving a speech on a controversial topic, you can expect to receive some tough questions.

Consult with the people in your business who work close to the news—for example, the consumer advocate, the treasurer, the public relations staff. Have them review your list of possible questions. Ask them to add to it.

Don't be intimidated by the difficulty of these questions. Don't allow yourself to be placed in a defensive position. Instead, come up with answers that work to *your* advantage. Practice these answers—*aloud.* It doesn't do any good to plan an assertive response if you can't sound assertive when you give it.

Here are ten practical tips to help you with a question-and-answer session:

1. *Take questions from all parts of the audience.*

2. *Listen carefully to each question.* Don't smile or frown excessively as you listen—save your response until it's time for you to answer. And don't nod your head enthusiastically to show you understand the question. The audience may think you automatically agree with the question.

3. *Pay attention to your posture and body language.* Avoid any fidgeting motions that might reveal anxiety. Never, for example, light up a cigarette while you are being asked a question.

4. *Treat every questioner as an equal.* Don't try to compliment someone by saying, "Good question." It implies the others were *not* good questions. Be especially careful not to "brush off" questions from your subordinates or to fawn over comments from your superiors.

5. *Repeat all positive questions.* This makes sure the audience has heard the question. It also buys you a few seconds of time to prepare your response.

6. *Paraphrase the negative questions.* This allows you to set the tone and to control the emphasis of your answer. *Don't* repeat any hostile language, e.g., "Why did we fire all the older workers who had been with the company for so many years?" If you repeat it, you might be quoted as actually saying it.

7. *Look first at the person who asked the question.* Then establish good eye contact with the whole audience as you give the answer.

8. *Respond simply and directly.* If your response is too long, the audience may think you're trying to stall for time to avoid further questions.

9. *Don't extend your answers.* The more you say, the more chance you have to hang yourself. Remember Calvin Coolidge: "I have never been hurt by anything I didn't say."

10. *Don't limit yourself by saying, "This will be our last question."* If that question turns out to be a difficult one and you handle it poorly, you will end in a needlessly weak position. Instead, try saying, "We have a few minutes left. Can I take another question?" If you feel confident with the answer you give, then let this be the last question and wrap up the session. If you aren't satisfied to end the session at this point, you still have the option of accepting another question.

How to Handle Special Problems in a Q&A Session

• *If no one asks you a question.* Don't just stand there in silence. Ask yourself a question. Try, "Last week, when

I spoke to the Chamber of Commerce, several people asked me about our plans to build a new plant. Perhaps I should spend a few minutes on that."

- *If someone asks about something you already discussed in the speech.* Answer anyway. Perhaps you didn't make your message clear enough. Try another approach. If you used an anecdote to explain something during your speech, use statistics or quotations to clarify the point during your Q&A. If the audience didn't understand your first technique, maybe they'll understand your second or third.

- *If someone repeats a question that's already been asked.* Don't answer it again. "I believe we've already answered that" will usually work.

- *If someone tries to turn a question into a long-winded speech.* Stop him or her politely but firmly. Interrupt the person's rambling and ask him or her to come to the point and give the question—"in the interest of saving time." The rest of the audience will appreciate this indication that you value their time. Gestures can help. When you interrupt the questioner, raise your hand in front of you. This "stop sign" signal will reinforce your words.

- *If someone asks a totally irrelevant question (perhaps about your personal life).* Just say, "Well, that's not what we're here to discuss." Period. End of discussion.

- *If someone asks a disorganized question.* Respond to only one part and ignore the rest. Naturally, pick the part of the question that will help you to reinforce your message.

- *If you don't know the answer.* Say so. Offer to get the information and send it to the person.

- *If you run out of time.* Say you're sorry you couldn't get to answer every question. Offer to make yourself availa-

ble to people who want to pursue the subject further—
perhaps during a coffee break or during a cocktail hour.

How to Respond to Hostile Questions

You're the manager of consumer conservation at an electric
utility, and you've just finished speaking to a community
group about energy-saving ideas. Up pops a hand, and you
hear this question: "How can you stand there and talk about
conservation when thousands of old people in your service
area are so poor that they can't even eat? What do you want
them to do? Pay high rates and eat cat food?"

How do you get out of this one? Very carefully.

Hostile questions are *not* impossible to answer. They just
require special skills. Learn the techniques and practice them.
Do it now, before you need to use these skills. Don't wait until
you're put on the spot. It's too late then.

Start by giving yourself three basic rights:

- the right to be treated fairly

- the right to stay in control—of yourself and the situation

- the right to get your message across correctly

Remember: You are the invited speaker. No one in the
audience has the right to take your role or to obscure your
message.

Concentrate on getting your message across. In preparation for any Q&A, choose two or three important points that
you can express as one-liners. Memorize these lines. Use them
as *focus statements* when the Q&A gets difficult.

Rephrase any hostile questions so you can get into a *focus
statement.*

For example:

Q: "All of your fancy plans to put up these big apartment buildings will just tear up our streets and tear down our old homes. What do you want to do to our downtown area? Kill it?"

A: "You're asking about our redevelopment plans." (rephrased question) *"Well, let me say that we plan to build a healthy downtown—where people can live and where businesses can do business."* (focus statement)

Don't be afraid of hostile questions. As Edmund Burke put it: "He who opposes me, and does not destroy me, strengthens me."

It's also imperative that you never insult anyone. "Well, I'd never insult anyone in a question-and-answer session. That would be mean. And dangerous." Is this what you're thinking to yourself?

You're right. It *would* be mean and dangerous to insult anyone during a Q&A. But unthinking speakers do it all the time. Let me share a few bad examples so you can learn from their lessons.

Q: "Why is the company authorizing so much stock? That's way too much!"

A: "Do you know the difference between issued and authorized stock? Issued stock is . . ."

Q: "Are you saying I don't know what I'm talking about!"

Don't accidentally insult a questioner's intelligence. Listen respectfully to the question, then try, "For the benefit of the whole audience, let me explain the difference between *issued* and *authorized* stock."

Q: "Why didn't you do more testing on that drug before you sold it to the public?"

  A: "If you'd been listening to my speech, you'd obviously
  know the answer to that question."

Don't embarrass questioners in public. They will never
forget the humiliation, and they will hold it against you.
 Warning: "Obviously" can be an emotionally charged
word. It often seems like a put-down. After all, if something
was so obvious, why did the questioner miss it? Is he or she
stupid?

A heckler dominated the Q&A session at an important
meeting. The speaker grew increasingly frustrated, and finally
threatened the heckler with, "I'm going to ask you to sit down
in a few minutes."
 Of course, the heckler just loved this attention, so he
continued to interrupt the Q&A with long-winded questions.
Each time, the speaker raised his voice and said, "I'm going to
ask you to sit down soon."
 Don't make idle threats. The heckler will love the extra
attention, and the audience will think you are ineffectual. If
you can't carry out a threat, don't make it.

  Q: "Why do you think your program is so much better
  than the one Fred Smith started, which we've been
  using for years?"

  A: "Well, there were lots of problems with the old program. For example, . . ."

Don't criticize a predecessor's work. Even if Fred is no
longer with the organization, he may have friends and rela-
tives and loyal supporters who still are. They will resent you
for knocking his work.
 Instead, explain that you inherited a fine structure, but
that new information, subsequent events, increased funding,
larger staff, or advanced technology allowed you to build on
that foundation. For a strong emotional appeal, point out

how Fred himself would have probably welcomed the chance to expand his original program: "At Fred's retirement dinner, he said the future seemed to be coming faster and faster—and that he wished he could be around to see all the changes in our industry."

Never give the impression that you've disregarded someone else's work, or the audience will think you are reckless and arrogant.

Tips for Television Interviews

In the age of soundbites, the three-minute Gettysburg Address would have been two-and-a-half minutes too long. One of today's ambitious young correspondents would probably have summed it up this way: "The President himself admitted to this subdued Pennsylvania crowd what his men have been saying privately: That no one will long remember what he said here."

—Richard M. Nixon

Television brings us a wide range of morning interview shows, evening news programs, the late-night news, special crisis reports, weekly news analyses, profiles of executives, coverage of community events, local business updates, hard-hitting exposés, consumer advisories, and insider stories.

Of course, to keep all this news coverage running, television needs *people who will appear as guests.* Question: Will *you* be sitting in one of those interview chairs someday?

There are two basic ways to appear on TV:

1. Perhaps you'll be invited to promote something you're proud of. Some common situations:

- An executive is eager to appear on TV so she can publicize a new sales effort.

- A civic leader needs visibility so he can create support for a worthwhile community project.

- A high-school principal welcomes the chance to talk about a unique educational experiment.

2. On the other hand, perhaps you'll be "summoned" to appear on a news program to defend, explain, or justify something that's potentially embarrassing to your organization. A sampling of crises:

- food tampering

- an airline crash

- a devastating fire

- drug abuse

- union corruption

- criminal activity

- employee layoffs

No matter whether you're "invited" or "summoned" to appear on TV . . . either way, you've got to come across to the viewing audience with credibility, clarity, and competence. These TV interview tips should help:

Before the interview

- *Set your objective.* Pick two or three key points you want to stress during the interview. Make them simple, powerful, and relevant.

- *Watch the program.* Observe the host's style. Is your interviewer generally friendly or antagonistic . . . probusiness or antibusiness . . . concise or long-winded . . . well-prepared or prone to wing it?

- *Ask about the format.* Length of interview? Taped or live? Other guests? Number and duration of commercials? Policy on call-ins?

- *Provide accurate information.* Make sure the producer has an accurate description of your credentials. Clarify the proper pronunciation of your name.

- *Anticipate likely questions.* The best way to do this: Put yourself in the interviewer's shoes, then imagine the questions *you'd* ask in that situation.

- *Prepare effective answers.* Be brief, be specific, be helpful. Use terms the audience will understand. Be prepared with anecdotes the audience will enjoy. Use real-life situations the audience can relate to. Practice your answers out loud, and tape-record them. Review the tapes: Cut any long parts, spice up any dull parts.

- *Pay attention to your appearance.* How you look will be as important as what you say, so dress appropriately for the occasion. (Again, it pays to watch the program in advance. Ask yourself: "How will my outfit look against *this* particular set?) In general, be neat and be conservative. Whatever you do, don't let your clothes overpower your message.

During the interview

- *Arrive early.* Face it: TV studios can be downright overwhelming. The glaring lights, the high-tech cameras, the multiple monitors, the hustle and bustle of assistant producers, the technicians' jargon . . . all potentially intimidating.

    So, don't arrive at the last minute. Give yourself a chance to look around and get familiar with all the sights and sounds. Then, you can put these distractions aside and focus on the *important* thing: giving a good interview!

- *Concentrate.* Once the interview starts, you must give it your concentrated attention. Really *listen* to the interviewer's questions. Above all, listen for opportunities where you can reinforce your main points.

- *Be clear.* Don't hem and haw. Don't ramble. Don't filibuster. Open your answer with a simple statement ("That's right," "No, not really," "Absolutely," "That's a common misconception," "Yes, it's true"), then add the necessary details to support your case.

- *Be human.* Tell a personal story. Give a quick case history. Share a recent example. Use a lively quotation or a revealing anecdote. Tap into the emotions of the audience.

  All of these techniques will help you come across as a believable, trustworthy, and caring individual.

- *Be conversational.* Leave your jargon back at your office. Keep your boring statistics locked in your briefcase.

- *Be helpful.* Try to approach the topic from the audience's perspective. Give examples they can relate to. Offer solutions they can put into practice.

- *Be visual.* Television is a visual medium. If you've got terrific film footage, or relevant documents, or startling photographs, or interesting objects, use them to your advantage.

- *Use appropriate body language.* Beware of "grand movements." Sure, they might look great when you're standing at the lectern on a big stage . . . but when you appear on a small TV screen in someone's bedroom, those same movements can make you look downright silly. Another caution: Avoid repeatedly nodding "yes" as your interviewer asks questions. Just listen . . . then let your response reflect your opinion.

- *Take advantage of commercial breaks.* Use this time to collect your thoughts, to do a mental rundown, to make sure you're getting in your basic points. Ask the host what's next—and even suggest a specific area you'd like to discuss (politely, of course).

- *Exude confidence.* After all, if *you* don't have faith in your own expertise, why should the audience?

- *Radiate charisma.* Sincerity and charm sell . . . and nowhere do they sell better than on TV. Remember that, and you can't go too wrong.

Final Observation: The Power of a Short Answer

One time, Barbara Bush made the risky comment that New York City mayor Ed Koch was "full of it."

Later, a reporter tried to grill her on this comment—wanting to know exactly what she meant, and no doubt hoping she'd stick her foot in her mouth.

With classic Barbara Bush wit, she simply smiled and gave this answer: "Joy."

Hard to do much better than that.

How to Handle Trick Questions

Questions often fall into patterns. If you recognize the pattern, you can get around the question much better.

Be aware of these trick questions:

- *The "A" or "B" Question.* "Which is more important to your company—building a new production plant in our town or opening new offices out-of-state?"

  Don't pigeonhole yourself. Say, "They're both important," or "Those are just two of our concerns."

- *The Multiple Question.* "Will the university make a special effort to recruit minority students? And will the athletic program be more closely supervised? And will you build any more student housing?"

Don't get confused by three or four questions at once. Answer only one.

- *The Open Question.* "Tell me about your company."

  Here is where it pays off to have preestablished *focus statements.* Use them to create the image you want.

- *The "Yes" or "No" Question.* "Will you have any lay-offs next year—yes or no?"

  Never get forced into a yes or no. Make the statement in your own words.

- *The Hypothetical Question.* "What if the union doesn't accept this offer?"

Avoid being pulled into "doomsday" situations. They're like bottomless pits. Cut off the discussion by saying, "We're confident we'll reach an agreement." Consider this exchange from a news conference with President Reagan:

Q: "Mr. President, if there's no change in the situation, is there a time when you would want to bring the troops home?"

A: "Let me just say that—I got into trouble a little while ago from trying to answer a hypothetical question with a hypothetical answer. And various interpretations were placed on it."

Reagan then avoided a hypothetical answer and gave a *focus statement* that summed up his position.

- *The Off-the-Record Question.* There is no such thing as an off-the-record question in a Q&A session. Answer all questions as though your answer will appear on the front page of tomorrow's paper. It just might!

- *The Ranking Question.* "Would you name the top three concerns of today's teaching profession?"

   Again, don't pigeonhole yourself. As soon as you name the top three concerns, someone will ask, "What's the matter? Don't you care about *(blank)?*" And then you'll be stuck. Instead, try, "Among our most important concerns are . . ."

- *The Nonquestion Question.* "I don't think we need all this new equipment."

   How can you respond to such a statement? By converting it into a question. For example: "I'm hearing an important question in your statement, and that question is, 'How can we benefit by using this equipment?' " Then, you can answer the question without having to rebut the original statement.

- *The False Premise Question.* "Now that you've dumped all that pollution into the river, how are you going to clean it up?"

   Always correct a false premise. Say in a firm voice, "That's not so. Let me set the record straight."

- *The Cross-Examination Question.* "Let's review the waste-disposal issue once again. What possible explanation can you give for this disgraceful situation?"

   If the questioner has sneaky motives, address them. Say, "That sounds like a trap. What are you trying to get me to say?" *Remember:* You are not in a courtroom. You do not have to subject yourself to a cross-examination.

What to Include in Your Answer

- *Cite your own professional experience.* "In my twenty-five years of work in this field, I have never seen anything like that."

- *Cite your own personal experience.* "Well, I just went out and bought a *(blank)*. I know the product's good."

- *Quote the experts.* "The top researchers in the country would disagree with you. At Columbia University, for example, . . ."

- *Present facts.* "The fact of the matter is . . ."

- *Disassociate.* "That's like comparing apples and avocados. We can't be compared."

- *Establish a bond.* "Well, I can certainly understand how you feel. In fact, many people have felt the same way. But when they became more familiar with the program, they found out that . . ."

- *Simplify the numbers.* "Yes, $10,000 *does* seem like a lot of money to spend on training until you consider that this amounts to only 'x' dollars per person. And increased productivity will pay back our initial investment in just one year."

- *Recognize the importance of the question.* Some people don't want an answer. They just want to be heard. They want their day in court. If you recognize this need for attention, you will satisfy them. Play psychologist and say in your most soulful voice, "Sounds like that's an important issue to you." But be careful not to sound patronizing.

- *Above all, include your focus statements.* Use those one-liners that will stick in the minds of the audience—and may be quoted by the press.

How to Use a Bridging Response

Use a *bridging response* when you don't want to discuss the question. Listen to the question, then bridge to one of your focus statements by saying something like this:

- "Well, Paul, the really important issue we should be discussing is . . ."

- "Consumers would be better off if they asked about . . ."

- "That's not the critical issue here. The critical issue is . . ."

In each case, use the bridging response to get into a specific point you want to make.

If possible, address the questioner by name. It produces a calming, persuasive effect.

Use Humor Sparingly—If at All

It's too easy for humor to backfire in a question-and-answer session. Why? Because it seems to be directed at a particular person. If you pick on someone whom the audience really likes, you're in trouble.

For example: "You'd better get to the point of your question because I'm only president of this organization for another eight months." Such a line might draw a laugh, but if you happen to say it to the wrong person, the audience may turn against you.

Of course, there's a flip side to this coin:

If a *questioner* says something funny, chuckle. Show you're human. Never try to top someone's line. Let that person have a brief, shining moment of glory. The audience will appreciate—and respond to—your good-naturedness.

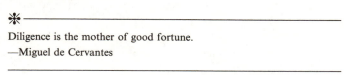

T E N

The Nitty-Gritty Details

❋ ————————————————————————————

Diligence is the mother of good fortune.
—Miguel de Cervantes

Why worry about giving a speech? You'll be much better off if you put your energy into thinking and planning. Think about the logistics of giving your speech. Plan for the unexpected and the unwanted. And prepare, prepare, prepare.

This chapter will show you how to:

- prepare *your speech* for delivery by typing the manuscript in an easy-to-read script format

- prepare *the room* by making the physical layout work for you, not against you

- prepare *yourself* by treating your voice and your body as valuable tools

HOW TO TYPE A SPEECH

Type your speech so that:

- it is easy for you to deliver

- it is easy for the press to read

- it is easy for a substitute speaker to deliver if you are unable to speak

Proper manuscript preparation takes some extra effort, but your efforts will pay off.

Here are twenty-one tips from the professionals:

1. Type the script in *speechwriter*. This is a large-size typeface designed especially for public speakers. Use upper and lower case.

2. If you don't have access to one of these special type-writing elements, just use your regular typewriter and type in all-caps so that the print is large enough for you to see. But be alert: When reading a speech typed with all caps, it is easy to confuse proper nouns with ordinary words.

3. Identify the speech on the top left corner of the first page with:
   YOUR NAME AND TITLE
   THE GROUP YOU'RE SPEAKING TO
   THE CITY YOU'RE SPEAKING IN
   THE DATE OF THE SPEECH

4. Double-space between lines. Triple-space between paragraphs.

5. Start typing the speech about four inches from the top of the first page. This gives you the space to make last-minute additions to your opening.

6. Be sure to end each line with a complete word. *Never* hyphenate words at the ends of lines. Leave the line short rather than hyphenate.

7. Don't break statistics at the end of a line. For example:

"At our company we spend five
hundred dollars a week on maintenance."

(When delivering this speech, you might accidentally say "five thousand dollars" and would have to correct yourself.)

8. End each page with a complete paragraph. It's too dangerous to start a sentence on one page and finish it on another. You can lose too much time while shifting the page.

9. Be sure to leave about three inches of white space at the bottom of *each* page. If you try reading copy that runs all the way to the bottom of the page, your head will go too far down, the audience won't be able to see your face, and your volume will decrease.

10. Leave wide margins at the left and right of the copy.

11. Number each page on the upper right.

12. Write out abbreviations (for example, M-B-A) with hyphens.

13. Spell out foreign words and names phonetically. For example, after "Mr. Chianese," write "Mr. Kee-uh-NAY-zee" in parentheses.

14. Don't use roman numerals in the script. They're fine for written presentations, but not speeches. It would sound stilted to say, "now, roman numeral one . . ."

15. Underline words or phrases that are to be emphasized.

16. Use three dots (. . .) to mark slight pauses. They are often useful at the end of a paragraph, to remind you to pause for a second before proceeding.

17. Mark longer pauses with two slash marks (/ /). These slash marks remind you to stop for a few seconds, either to give the audience time to laugh or to give you time to change the direction of your speech. If

you use slash marks, be sure to drop down a couple of lines before you start typing again.

Like this. Otherwise, you'll obscure the marks.

18. At the end of the speech, include an address where people can write for more information.

19. Never staple the pages of your speech together. Simply fasten them with a paper clip, which can be easily removed when you're ready to speak.

20. Place the manuscript in a plain, dark folder—ready for your delivery.

21. Always prepare a spare copy and carry it separately. For example, if you're going to deliver an out-of-town speech, carry one copy in your briefcase and another in your suitcase.

Caution: None of these rules will help you much if you forget to bring the speech along—or, if you mistakenly grab another document on your way to the lectern.

In England years ago, a vice-admiral stood up to speak to the Royal Navy Old Comrades Association. After taking a careful second look at his notes, he was forced to end even before he began.

His confession to the puzzled audience? "By mistake, I brought a shopping list my wife gave me."

HOW TO PREPARE THE ROOM

It's amazing how many good speeches have been ruined by a nonfunctioning microphone or by miserable lighting or by a poor ventilating system.

You may have prepared a wise and witty speech, but if

the audience can't hear you or see you, who cares? And if the audience is suffering from an air-conditioning system that doesn't work, you might as well wrap it up early and head home.

Check out the room before you speak. If you can't go in person, ask someone else to look at it. Or telephone the person who invited you to speak. Ask some basic questions:

- *Does the room have windows?* Even more importantly, do the windows have heavy drapes? You'll need to close them if you show any slides.

  You'll also need to close the drapes if you're speaking in a motel conference room that looks onto a swimming pool. There's *no way* you can compete with beautiful, firm bodies in scanty bathing wear, so shut those drapes before the audience arrives and save yourself a lot of frustration during the speech.

- *Is there a lectern?* Does it have a light? Is it plugged in and ready to go? Is a spare bulb handy?

  Does the lectern have a shelf underneath where you can keep a glass of water, a handkerchief, a few cough drops?

  Can the lectern be adjusted to the proper height? If you're short, is there a box to stand on? Move everything into place *before* you arrive at the lectern to speak.

- *Can you be heard without a microphone?* If so, don't use one.

- *Is the public address system good?* Test it and ask an assistant to listen to you. Must you stoop or lean to reach the microphone? It should be pointed at your chin. Can you be heard in all corners of the room? Is the volume correct? Do you get feedback? Where do you turn the microphone on and off?

- *How about the lighting?* Do a "test run" with the house lights. Do they create a glare when you look at the audience? In general, the light level on you should be about the same as the light level on the audience. Does a crystal chandelier hanging over your head create a glare for the audience? Remove the bulbs. Will the spotlight appear where it should? Adjust it.

- *What about the seating?* After they've taken off their coats and seated themselves and gotten comfortable, people hate to be asked to move. Perhaps it reminds them of school days. Be sure to arrange the seating to your advantage *before* the audience arrives.

  Will people be seated at round dining tables, with some of their backs to you? If so, allow time for them to shuffle their seats before you start to speak.

  It's too difficult to maintain eye contact when listeners are scattered around a large room. If you expect a small crowd, try to remove some of the chairs before the audience arrives. Do anything you can to avoid "gaps" in the audience where energy can dissipate.

  If you'll speak in a large auditorium, have the rear seats roped off. This forces the audience to sit closer to you. This roped-off area is also great for latecomers. They can slip in without disturbing the rest of the audience.

  If only a few people show up, move your lectern from the stage to floor level to create more intimacy. The closer you are to your listeners, and the closer your listeners are to each other, the more successful you will be.

- *Is there good ventilation?* Can the air-conditioning system handle large crowds? Can the heat be regulated?

  Hotels are notoriously stuffy. One time I had to give a speech at a big hotel in New York City, and when I arrived, I found the room temperature had been set at eighty degrees. I immediately pushed the thermostat way back—and by the time the audience arrived, the room was comfortable.

Rule: Always arrive well ahead of your audience, so you can make these necessary changes more easily.

- *How many doors lead into the room?* Can you lock the doors at the front of the room to prevent intruders from upstaging you? Can you have assistants posted at the rear doors to ensure quiet entrances from latecomers and quiet exits from people who must leave before you finish?

- *Is music being "piped" into the room?* If so, turn it off immediately. Do not rely on hotel staff to do so when it's your time to speak.

- *Is the room soundproof?* This becomes a critical issue when you speak in a hotel room. Who knows what will be happening in the room next to yours: a raucous bachelor party, a pep rally, or an enthusiastic sales pitch. What audience would concentrate on, say, cogeneration if they could listen to the excitement happening next door?

  Don't take any chances. If possible, make an unannounced visit to the hotel to check things out for yourself. Hotel managers always say their conference rooms are "nice and quiet." Trust them about as far as you could throw the hotel.

  If you find that sound carries through the walls, speak to the manager. Ask to have the adjacent rooms empty during your speech. If the hotel is booked solid, they won't be able to accommodate this request, but it doesn't hurt to ask.

- Above all, get the name and telephone number of a maintenance person who can step right in and replace a fuse or a lightbulb, or adjust the air conditioner. Keep this person's name and number handy at all times.

Emerson was right. *Shallow* men believe in luck.

HOW TO USE AUDIOVISUAL AIDS

More speeches are ruined by audiovisual aids than are improved by them. I caution all speakers to be especially careful here. Don't ruin a first-rate speech with audiovisual materials that are second-rate, or even unnecessary.

A-V aids are unnecessary if they:

- contribute no new information to your speech

- fail to help the audience understand or appreciate your message

- actually *detract* from your role as speaker

Unfortunately, most speakers use audiovisual aids as a "crutch." An all-too-common example:

The speaker says, "I want to tell you about our new accounting system," and then flashes a slide that reads "New Accounting System."

Does this slide contribute any new information? No. Does this slide really help the audience to understand the speaker's message? No. Does this slide detract from the speaker's presence? Unfortunately, yes.

Speeches are designed primarily for the ear, but visuals are designed for the eye. If you are trying to talk while people are looking at visual aids, rather than at you, your words won't be as powerful. Your eye contact with the audience won't be as strong. In short, your message won't be as effective.

Need convincing? Try holding an important conversation on the telephone while looking at a television show. How much information will you miss?

If you really need to use audiovisual aids—to simplify

complex information or to create an emotional appeal—use them wisely.

One effective technique is to use an audiovisual "insert." Prepare a short slide show or a videotape and insert this into your speech as a self-contained unit. The audience can concentrate on the audiovisual segment and then return concentration to the remainder of your speech.

Here are some suggestions for effective audiovisual inserts:

Slides

- Set written copy flush left, with a ragged right margin.

- Keep type uniform. Sans-serif type takes enlargement very well. Avoid enlarged typewriter letters.

- Use upper and lower case, not all-capital, letters.

- Use normal spacing between words and caps.

- Keep headings uniform. Use smaller sizes on subheads to indicate relative importance.

- Use only a few lines of type on any slide.

- Use color on charts and graphs to add interest.

- Double-check everything to make sure it is in proper order.

- Make the room as dark as possible.

- Use a screen, not a wall. Make sure the screen is large enough for everyone to see.

- Everything on a slide must be visible to the people in the last row. Take a look at your visuals from the back of the room.

- Tape down the projector cord so no one will trip on it.

- Make sure the projector and screen are properly aligned.

- Leave each slide on the screen long enough for everyone to read and understand it and for you to make your point, then move on to the next one. The audience's interest will flag if a slide is left on too long.

Videotapes

- Don't be afraid to use emotional appeal. Videotapes are uniquely suited to offering "slice of life" material. For example, if you're giving a speech on the need to donate blood, try a short videotape showing the people who benefit from blood donations. Get close-ups of faces, of children holding their parents' hands, of doctors comforting patients. Don't use "perfect" people. Use "real" people who look like your audience.

- Make sure the tapes are compatible with the available playback units.

- Have enough monitors available. The audience should not have to strain to see your videotape.

- Check and adjust each monitor in advance.

Audiotapes

- Audiotapes are excellent for presenting new radio jingles, public service announcements, or short messages from focus groups—to name just a few uses.

- Jack your playback unit directly into the room's sound system.

Flip Charts

Remember how effectively General Norman Schwarzkopf used flip charts during the briefings for Desert Storm? No wishy-washy overhead transparencies for "Stormin' Norman."

General Schwarzkopf used neat, simple, understated flip charts. And, in doing so, he ushered in "the era of the chart" in corporate America.

Alas, while many business leaders have adopted the use of flip charts, they have failed to use them as effectively as the general. Perhaps these guidelines will help:

- Use flip charts only with small groups. (What's the sense in showing a chart that can't be read beyond the third row?)

- Keep your lettering clear, bold, brief, and horizontal.

- Avoid using more than three or four curves on any graph—particularly if the curves cross one another. (Otherwise, you'll present something that resembles a splattering of spaghetti.)

- Differentiate between curves by using various thicknesses and patterns. For your most important curve, use a bold line. For the next in importance, use a light line. For the third, use a series of dashes. For the least important, use a series of dots.

- Don't turn your back to the audience when you refer to the flip charts.

- If you point out something particular on the chart, be sure you're pointing accurately. (Try to avoid the befuddled weatherman syndrome. You know what I mean . . . when the TV weatherman refers to a blizzard in Wisconsin, but carelessly waves his pointer somewhere around Arkansas. This is hardly a way to inspire confidence in any audience.)

- If you're going to write on your flip charts in front of the audience, make sure ahead of time that you've got several working markers. (President Reagan once got stuck with a grease pencil that failed to function. And, I remember watching an otherwise competent manager grow increasingly flustered when his first marker proved dry . . . and the replacement proved dry, as well.)

Objects

Want to show off an interesting object, or hold up an unusual item, or share a powerful photo? Fine—just make sure everyone can see what you've got.

- First, lift it up in the air.
- Hold it steady for a few moments.
- Then, move it slowly so everyone in the room has time to see it. (Be quiet while you're moving the object. Let people look at it in silence. Otherwise, they won't be paying full attention to your words. Even worse, once the object is out of their view, they'll feel they're missing something if they continue to hear you explaining the item.)

Emergency A-V Kit

Even with careful preparation, lots of things can go wrong when you use audiovisual materials. Prepare an emergency kit and carry it to all presentations. Include:

- extension cords
- spare light bulbs
- three-pronged adapters
- a multiple-outlet box
- masking tape
- scissors, screwdriver, pliers
- a small flashlight

After all, a speech that cost thousands to prepare can be ruined by the failure of a $1.19 light bulb. Prevent failure. Prepare carefully.

HOW TO PREPARE YOURSELF

When you give a speech, you want to look your best, sound your best, and feel your best. Don't leave these things to chance.

How to Look Your Best

Don't wear brand-new clothes to give a speech. New clothes haven't had a chance to "fit" your body. They often feel stiff and uncomfortable, and what could be worse than having a button pop off or a seam rip open when you gesture in the middle of your speech? Wear "old favorites" instead—clothes that fit well and move the way *you* move.

Dress conservatively for most business functions. If in doubt about the suitability of a piece of clothing, don't wear it. Your appearance should not interfere with your message.

For men: A dark suit—clean and well-pressed, of course. (Navy blue or "banker's" blue is generally a color that conveys authority and elicits trust.) A long-sleeved shirt. (White or blue look best under bright lights.) A conservative tie with a touch of red for power (an old politician's trick). Long, dark socks. (The audience shouldn't see a patch of hairy leg when you sit down and cross your legs.) Well-shined shoes. No pens sticking out of your shirt pocket, please. And no coins or keys bulging in your pants pockets.

For women: A suit or a dress (static-free and noncling, of course). No low necklines. Be especially careful with your hemline if you will be seated on stage before you speak. Moderate heels—no spiked heels that will clomp as you cross a wooden floor. And no rattling jewelry. Arrange to leave your purse with someone in the audience. Do not carry it to the podium.

How to Sound Your Best

Treat your voice well. No cheering for the local football team the day before.

Try using a humidifier the night before. If you're staying in a hotel room, fill the bathtub with water before going to sleep. Moisture in the air will help prevent a dry-throat feeling.

Hot tea with honey and lemon is great for the voice. Use herbal tea for an extra calming effect. Chamomile tea can be particularly relaxing.

How to Feel Your Best

On the day before a big speech:

- Don't decide to get a totally new hairstyle. What would happen if you hated it?

- Don't decide to start that intensive exercise program you've been talking about for months. A brisk walk around the park? Fine. A five-mile run? Insane. Who wants aches and pains to deal with on top of everything else?

- Don't decide to "paint the town red." Wait until *after* the speech to celebrate. You'll feel better about yourself.

Delivery

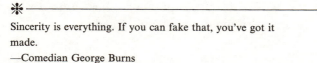

Sincerity is everything. If you can fake that, you've got it
made.
—Comedian George Burns

Practice makes perfect, the saying goes. Well, practice may not
make you a perfect speaker, but it will certainly make you a
better speaker. With the right coaching, you may even become
a great speaker.

This chapter will coach you on:

- executive presence

- voice control

- eye contact

- body language

It will also show you how to deal with two special concerns: nervousness and hecklers.

PRACTICING YOUR DELIVERY

Practice your *delivery,* not just your speech.

It's not enough to know the *content* of your speech. You

must also be comfortable with the gestures and pauses and emphases that will help get your message across to the audience.

To do this, practice the speech in six stages. First, familiarize yourself with the script itself. Then familiarize yourself with the delivery techniques you'll need.

1. *Begin by reading the speech aloud to yourself.* Tape-record it. How long does it take? Where do you need to pause to avoid running out of breath in mid-sentence? Should you rewrite any sentences so they're easier to deliver? Do you need to vary your pace?

   How does your voice sound? Does it fade at the end of sentences?

   If you generally have trouble projecting your voice, try putting the tape recorder across the room while you practice. This trick should *force* you to speak louder.

2. *Deliver the speech standing in front of a mirror.* By now, you should be familiar enough with the material to look up from the manuscript fairly often. Concentrate on emphasizing the right parts. See how your face becomes more animated at certain points in the speech.

   Caution: Be sure to rehearse the entire speech each time you practice. Otherwise, you'll have a well-prepared beginning but a weak ending.

   Deny yourself the luxury of "backtracking." If you make a mistake during rehearsal—trip on a line or leave something out—don't go back and start again. Be realistic. How would you recover from a mistake in front of an audience? That's how you should recover from it during your rehearsal.

3. *Deliver the speech to a friend.* Try to simulate a realistic environment. Stand up. Use a lectern. Arrange some chairs.

   If you need to put on glasses to see the script, now's the time to practice doing that unobtrusively.

Practice moving the pages quietly to the side. Don't "flip" them over. Look at your listener.

By this point, you should have memorized the first fifteen seconds of your speech and the last fifteen seconds, moments when eye contact is most critical. Do *not* try to memorize the rest of the speech, or your delivery will sound stilted. Focus on the ideas, not the words. Just look up a lot to make sure you're getting those ideas across. It's this eye contact with an audience that animates a speaker.

Allow yourself to smile when it feels natural. Gesture with your hand to make a point. Let your face talk, too.

4. *Practice again before a small group.* Try to make good eye contact with each person. Play with your voice a little bit to keep your listeners' attention. Notice where it helps to speak faster, slower, louder, softer.

5. *Give it your best shot.* Consider this advice from Lord Chesterfield:

"Aim at perfection in everything, though in most things it is unattainable. However, they who aim at it and persevere, will come much nearer to it than those whose laziness and despondency make them give it up as unattainable."

6. *If possible, practice on-site.* You'll feel more confident in a room that seems familiar. If you can't practice on-site, be sure to arrive extra early so you can get comfortable with the layout of the room before you begin your speech.

PRESENCE

A speech doesn't start when you begin to speak. It starts the moment you enter the room.

An audience will start to form an opinion of you as soon as they see you. First impressions count. Make yours good.

Carry yourself with presence from the moment you arrive. Be well groomed. Don't carry loose papers. Walk in a brisk, businesslike manner. Be polite to receptionists and secretaries. They may tell their bosses about you later. It's fruitless to talk to an audience about corporate ethics if they've heard you be rude to the receptionist.

Listen carefully to other speakers and respond appropriately. Pay particular attention to the person who introduces you.

All eyes will be on you as you walk to the podium, so don't be buttoning your jacket or sorting your papers. Take care of those details *before* you leave your chair.

Don't bother to hide the fact that you'll use a written text. Just carry the speech at your side—not in front of your chest, where it looks like a protective shield. If you plan to shake hands with the person who introduced you, carry the speech in your other hand so you don't have to make a last-minute switch.

Never place your speech on the lectern in advance. Someone speaking ahead of you might carry it away accidentally, and then you'd be stuck.

When you get to the lectern, take care of "The Big Six"—preparations you can't afford to skip.

1. Open your folder and remove the paper clip from your speech.

2. Make sure the lectern is at a comfortable level. You should, of course, have adjusted it in advance, but if another speaker has changed the height, now's the time to correct it.

3. Check the position of the microphone. Again, you should have tested the microphone in advance. Check

the switch. If you question the level, just say, "Testing—one, two, three." *Do not blow into the microphone or tap it.*

4. Stand straight and place your weight evenly over both feet. This will help you feel "grounded" and in control of the situation.

5. *Look* at the audience before you start to speak. This pause will quiet them and give you a chance to . . .

6. . . . Breathe!
   Now, you're ready to speak.

VOICE

Demosthenes, the Athenian orator, supposedly practiced speaking with a mouthful of pebbles. You don't have to go to such extremes.

When you rehearse your speech, check these basics:

- *Rate.* Time yourself with a stopwatch. How many words do you speak in a minute? Most people speak in public at about 150 words per minute.

- *Variety.* Can you vary your pace? Slower to set a particular mood? Faster to create excitement?

- *Emphasis.* Do you emphasize the right words and phrases?

- *Volume.* Can people hear you? If not, open your mouth more.

- *Rhythm.* Do all your sentences sound alike? Do you habitually drop your voice at the end of a sentence?

- *Fillers.* Do you ruin the flow of your thoughts with "uh" and "er" and "ah"?

- *Clarity.* Do you slur your contractions (*wu'nt* for *wouldn't*)? Do you reverse sounds (*per*scription for *pre*scription)? Do you omit sounds (lis*t*s)?; Do you add sounds (acros*t*)?

If you have serious speech problems, get professional help. Many colleges and universities have excellent speech clinics. Take advantage of them.

EYE CONTACT

Good eye contact will do more to help your delivery than anything else.

When you *look* at people, they believe you care about them. They believe you are sincere. They believe you are honest. How can you go wrong if an audience feels this way about you?

Really *look* at the people in your audience—and look at them as *individuals.* Don't look over their heads or stare at some vague spot in the back of the room. Don't "sweep" the room with your eyes. Instead, look directly at one person until you finish a thought, then move on to another. You must maintain good eye contact with the audience if you are going to convey sincerity.

Avoid looking repeatedly at the same person. It's best to look at as many individuals as possible in the time allowed.

Eye contact will also give you instantaneous feedback. Does the audience look interested or are they nodding out? If you sense boredom, intensify your eye contact, vary your voice, use body language.

Try not to look up at the audience during grammatical pauses (for example, between sentences) because physical movement seems awkward when there's nothing verbal going on.

BODY LANGUAGE

Most books on public speaking talk about the importance of gestures. I prefer to talk about the importance of *body language*. It is, of course, important to gesture with your hands if you want to make a point. But it's just as important to speak *with your whole body.*

A raised eyebrow, a smile, a shrug of the shoulders—they all make a statement. If you use them wisely, they can contribute a lot to your speech.

If you watched TV during Operation Desert Shield and Desert Storm, you could learn a number of things about effective—and ineffective—delivery.

Case in point: General H. Norman Schwarzkopf. Remember those powerful briefing sessions?

- He stood tall—generally *beside* the lectern (in contrast to many corporate speakers, who hide behind their lecterns for dear life).

- He made bold gestures, and he made them away from the body—easy for all to see.

- He kept direct eye contact with the audience.

- And—refreshing in a military authority!—he used facial expressions to convey a wide variety of emotions: determination, sympathy, pride, anger, commitment. (No stone-faced bureaucrat, here.)

In sharp contrast, think back to the televised speeches made by King Hussein of Jordan. You may recall that he kept a rather annoying smile glued to his face. Even when he discussed the most serious of topics, his face was frozen into that artificial smile.

I call this affliction "the Jimmy Carter syndrome"—the

constant use of a smile, no matter how inappropriate. Avoid this syndrome like the plague. Smiles are effective only when they're natural, and when they really mean something.

It's not necessary (or even advisable) to choreograph your body movements in advance. You'll find that they spring naturally from your message, from your belief in what you're saying. If you put energy and thought and life into your message, your body movements will take good care of themselves. If you *don't*, no amount of hand-waving will help your cause.

As you rehearse and deliver your speech:

- You'll find yourself leaning forward slightly to make a stronger point.

- You'll find yourself smiling when you quote something amusing.

- You'll find yourself gesturing with your whole arm, not just with a finger or a flick of the wrist.

- You'll find yourself nodding slightly when you sense a good response from the audience.

- You'll find yourself shaking your head when you cite something that's offensive or inaccurate.

You'll find yourself, in short, developing charisma. The more energy you *give* to an audience, the more charisma you will develop. It's an exchange—you give and you get.

A word of caution about gestures. No feeble ones, please. If you raise just a finger to make a point, the audience may not even see the gesture. Raise your whole hand. Raise your whole arm. Make your movements *say* something.

If you have trouble expressing yourself physically, swing your arms in figure-eights before you speak. (In privacy, of course.) This big movement will loosen you up.

WHEN YOU FINISH SPEAKING

You've just spoken the last word of your speech. *Be careful.* Your speech isn't really over. Don't walk away from the podium yet. Hold your position. Look directly at the audience for a few more seconds. Remain in control of the silence just as you remained in control of the speech.

If you wrote a good speech, your final words were strong and memorable. In fact, your ending was probably the best part of the whole speech. Allow it to sink in.

Then, close your folder and walk away from the podium. Walk briskly and confidently—the same way you approached the podium.

When you take your seat, do *not* start talking to the person next to you. Someone else is probably at the podium now, and the audience would think it rude for you to be talking.

Above all, don't say things like, "Whew, am I glad *that's* over," or "Could you see how much my hands were trembling?" I have even seen speakers sit down and roll their eyes and shake their heads—a sure way to detract from an otherwise good speech.

Just sit quietly. Look attentive and confident.

There may well be applause. Smile and look pleased to be there. It would seem unnatural to act any other way.

Some speakers—those with a lot at stake—even plan their applause. They make sure that staff members attend the speech—not sitting together, but spread throughout the audience. When these people start to applaud, they produce a ripple effect. *Voilà!* A standing ovation!

NERVOUSNESS

"I'm afraid I'll be nervous."

That's a common feeling, and in some ways it's healthy.

It shows you care about getting your message across to the audience. You really *do* want to look and sound good.

But it's important to understand what nervousness is. Nervousness is simply *energy*. If you channel that energy, you can turn it into a positive force. You can make it work for you. You can use the extra energy to your advantage.

But if you allow that energy to go unchecked—if you allow *it* to control *you*—then you're going to have problems. A dry mouth, perhaps, or a cracking voice. Lots of rocking back and forth on your feet, or lots of "uh's" and "um's." Maybe even forgetfulness.

How can you channel your nervous energy?

By taking the advice that appears in this chapter. Learn to direct your extra energy into eye contact, body language, vocal enthusiasm. These physical activities provide an outlet for your nervousness. They offer a way to use up some of that extra energy.

What's more, good eye contact, strong body language, and vocal enthusiasm will build your *confidence*. It's hard to feel insecure when you look directly at your listeners and see the responsiveness in their faces.

Prespeech Tricks to Prevent Nervousness

There are tricks to every trade, and public speaking is no exception. Do what the pros do to keep their nervousness in check.

- *Try physical exercises.*

  Just before you speak, go off by yourself (to the restroom or to a quiet corner) and concentrate on the part of your body that feels most tense. Your face? Your hands? Your stomach? Deliberately tighten that part even more until it starts to quiver, then let go. You will feel an enormous sense of relief. Repeat this a few times.

Drop your head. Let your cheek muscles go loose and let your mouth go slack.

Make funny faces. Puff up your cheeks, then let the air escape. Or open your mouth and your eyes wide, then close them tightly. Alternate a few times.

Yawn a few times to loosen your jaw and your mucous membranes.

Pretend you're an opera singer. Try "mi, mi, mi" a few times. Wave your arms as you do it.

- *Try mental exercises.*

Picture something that's given you pleasant memories. Sailing on a blue-green ocean. Swimming in a mountain lake. Walking on a beach, feeling the sand between your toes. (Water often has a calming effect on people.)

- *Try a rational approach.*

Say to yourself, "I'm prepared. I know what I'm talking about." Or, "I've spent a year working on this project. Nobody knows as much about this project as I do." Or, "I'm glad I can talk to these people. It will help my career."

I know someone who repeats to herself, "This is better than death, this is better than death." That may sound extreme, but it works for her. And, she's right. Giving a speech *is* better than death.

If you're scared to give a speech, try to think of something that's *really* frightening. The speech should seem appealing by comparison.

- *Try a test run.*

Visualize exactly what will happen after you're introduced. You'll get out of your chair, you'll hold the folder in your left hand, you'll walk confidently across the stage, you'll hold your head high, you'll look directly at the person who introduced you, you'll shake his or her hand, you'll . . .

If you see yourself as confident and successful in your mental test run, you'll be confident and successful in your delivery.

Above all, never *say* that you're nervous. If you do, you'll make yourself more nervous. And you'll make the audience nervous, too.

During-the-Speech Tricks to Overcome Nervousness

Okay. You've prepared your speech carefully. You've done the prespeech exercises. Now you're at the podium and—can that be?—your mouth goes a little dry.

Don't panic. Just intensify your eye contact. Looking at the audience will take away your self-preoccupation and reduce the dryness.

Persistent dryness? Help yourself to the glass of water that you've wisely placed at the lectern. Don't be embarrassed. Say to yourself, "It's my speech, and I can damned well drink water if I want to."

What else can go wrong because of misplaced nervous energy? I once found that my teeth got so dry, my lips actually stuck to them. An actor friend later told me to rub a light coating of Vaseline over my teeth. It's a good tip.

Other minitraumas?

- *Sweat rolling off your forehead.* Wipe it away with the big cotton handkerchief that you also placed at the lectern. Don't hesitate to really *wipe*. Little dabs are ineffectual, and you'll have to dab repeatedly. Do it right the first time, and get it over with. Also, avoid using tissues. They can shred and get stuck on your face—not a terribly impressive sight.

- *A quavery voice.* Again, intensify your eye contact. Focus on *them*. Then lower your pitch and control your breath as you begin to speak. Concentrate on speaking distinctly and slowly.

- *Shaking hands.* Take heart. The audience probably can't see your trembling hands, but if they're distracting you, then use some body movement to diffuse that nervous energy. Change your foot position. Lean forward to make a point. Move your arms. (If your body is in a frozen position, your shaking will only grow worse.)

- *A pounding heart.* No, the audience *cannot* see the rising and falling of your chest.

- *Throat clearing.* If you have to cough, cough—away from the microphone. Drink some water, or pop a cough drop into your mouth. Again, the well-prepared speaker has an unwrapped cough drop handy at all times—and ready to use.

- *Runny nose, watery eyes.* Bright lights can trigger these responses. Simply pause, say "Excuse me," blow your nose or wipe your eyes, and get on with it. Don't make a big deal over it by apologizing. A simple "Excuse me" is just fine.

- *Nausea.* You come down with a viral infection two days before your speech and you're afraid of throwing up in the middle of it. Well, that's why they make antinausea drugs. Ask your doctor about a prescription.

    For actors, the show must always go on . . . even with serious viral infections. More than one actor has placed a trash can backstage so he could throw up between acts. But *you* are not an actor, and you really don't have to put yourself through this test of will power. If you are terribly ill—as opposed to being just mildly nervous—cancel your engagement. Since you've prepared a complete manuscript, perhaps a colleague could substitute for you. If substitution is not possible, offer to speak at a later date.

- *Burping.* Some people feel they have to burp when they get nervous. If you are one of these people, do plenty of physical relaxation exercises before you speak. Don't drink any carbonated beverages that day, and eat only a light lunch.

- *Fumbled words.* Professional speakers, radio announcers, and television anchorpeople fumble words fairly often. Someone once introduced President Reagan with this slip of the tongue: "Everyone who is for abortion was at one time a feces [sic]." So, why should *you* expect to be perfect?

  If it's a minor fumble, just ignore it and keep going.

  If it's a big one, fix it. Simply repeat the correct word—with a smile, to show you're human.

  Continue with your speech, but slow down a little bit. Once you've had a slip of the tongue, chances are high you'll have another. A fumble is a sort of symptom that you're focusing more on yourself than on your message. Relax and slow down.

- *Forgetfulness.* Some people look at an audience and forget what they want to say. Aren't you glad you made the effort to prepare a good written manuscript? It's all right there, so you have one less thing to worry about.

HECKLERS

> As a goose is not frightened by cackling nor a sheep by
> bleating, so do not let the clamor of a senseless multitude
> alarm you.
> —Epictetus

Hecklers tend to exist only in the bad dreams of speakers. They almost never pose real-life problems.

But if you are in the middle of your speech and you see someone waving an arm at you, then you need real-life help. And fast.

First of all, stay calm. Hecklers are like people who make obscene telephone calls. They just love to upset you. If you stay calm, you destroy their pleasure. If you stay calm, you also stay in control.

Ignore the hand that's waving in the air and keep right on speaking. It takes a lot of energy to wave a hand in the air, and the person will probably grow tired and give up. (Try waving your hand in the air for a few minutes, and you'll see what I mean.)

If you hear a voice? Stop speaking, remain calm, and ask the person to hold the question until after your speech. Be polite but firm. The audience will respect your approach and the person will most likely respect your request. Proceed with your speech.

If the person gets louder, you should *not* continue. Look instead at the person who organized this speaking engagement. If you're lucky, that person will come to your aid and quiet the heckler or escort him out of the room.

If not, speak to the heckler again. Say, "As I said before, I'll be glad to answer all questions *after* my speech." By now, your patience and professionalism should have earned the respect—and sympathy—of the rest of the audience.

If the heckling worsens, confront the person. Say, "Everyone here knows I'm *(name)* and I'm from the *(name)* company. Could you tell us who *you* are?" Hecklers, like obscene phone callers, almost certainly prefer to remain anonymous.

If the tirade continues, you will have to count on the audience for their support. Stop speaking, and step back from the podium. Let *them* put pressure on the heckler to shut up or leave.

After all, *you* are the invited speaker, not the heckler. You shouldn't have to justify your presence. You have a right to be treated fairly and to get your message across. If the audience isn't willing to support your basic rights, then don't waste your time trying to speak to them.

Leave—with dignity.

Of course, not everyone handles hecklers well.

- When Soviet President Mikhail Gorbachev was jeered at a May Day parade in Red Square, he seemed absolutely startled by the protestors' angry display.

- When President Miguel de la Madrid of Mexico tried to inaugurate the world soccer championship in Aztec Stadium, he was embarrassed to find his words utterly drowned out by whistles and boos.

- When Israeli Prime Minister Yitzak Shamir tried to eulogize a settler killed in the West Bank, he seemed unable to stop the hundreds of angry mourners who booed and cursed him. By the end of his muffled speech, he was pale and frowning.

However, with good preparation and a sharp mind, you might even be able to face a heckler and turn the situation to your advantage.

During the 1988 presidential election campaign, vice presidential candidate Senator Lloyd Bentsen ran into a noisy bunch of antiabortion protestors and was repeatedly interrupted by shouts.

Finally, the senator put his text aside and spoke directly—and powerfully—to the protestors.

He cited his visit that very morning at a children's hospital, where medical care had saved the lives of thousands of premature and handicapped babies.

He spoke of his role as chairman of the Adoption Caucus in the U.S. Senate—and he proudly told of being the parent of an adopted son. "We have done everything we can to ensure better medical care for our children everywhere."

By this time, the audience rose to its feet and applauded the senator. Seizing the momentum and capitalizing on audience support, he continued by making this blast at his opponent:

"Dan Quayle, you know he voted against child immunization, he voted against child nutrition, he voted against the school lunch program."

In doing so, Senator Bentsen took the negative experience of being heckled and turned it into a chance to drive home his message.

Here are two other techniques that have calmed hecklers:

- When Czechoslovakia's President Vaclav Havel found his speech disrupted by a large crowd of Slovak nationalists, the "Prague Spring" hero of 1968, Alexander Dubcek, rose to rebuke the hecklers for their behavior:

    "I know that you are drunk from freedom, but if this is the expression of democracy, we should be ashamed. We have not been fighting against one totalitarianism so that another can come in. It's not civilized to prevent presidents from speaking."

    And, with this rebuke, the hecklers were largely silenced.

- When Governor Mario Cuomo introduced New York City Mayor Ed Koch at a rally in support of state-supported housing, many elderly people in the crowd booed.

    The governor stopped their booing by taking this approach:

    "Hey, wait a minute. Wait a minute. You want to do me a favor, please? The mayor of the City of New York, Ed Koch, is one of the strongest voices we have on this Mitchell–Lama [housing] bill. How do you feel about him on *this* issue?"

The boos soon turned to cheers . . . and the mayor was able to step to the podium with his head high.

Whatever you do, try to avoid the response that Washington Mayor Marion Barry made when faced with hecklers at a neighborhood festival. The embattled D.C. mayor simply shot back with an obscene gesture—hardly the way to create an image of leadership.

T W E L V E

Media Coverage

Looking at yourself through the media is like looking at
one of those rippled mirrors in an amusement park.
—Edmund S. Muskie, U.S. Secretary of State

Your speech probably won't merit coverage on network television news, but there are lots of other ways to get good publicity for your speech.

Start small and work your way up the publicity scale.
Begin with the basics and do as much as your budget and your
time will allow—and, yes, as much as your *material* will allow.

Face it. Not all speeches are newsworthy. If you expect
the media to pay attention to a routine speech, you will be
disappointed.

Here are nine ways to get good publicity for your speech:

1. *Give it a catchy title.*   Come up with titles that *beg* to
   be quoted.

   Need ideas? Try variations on the titles of popular
   movies, books, and songs. Be specific. Be graphic. Be
   irreverent if you want. Just don't be boring.

   Consider these examples:

- "Dreams, Dollars and Deeds: The Sacred Fire and
  Health Access in America" (by John Tupper, M.D.,

American Medical Association, at AMA Annual Meeting)

- "Advice from an S.O.B.: Thrive or Die" (by Allen Neuharth, Gannett Foundation, to Society of Professional Journalists)

- "The Class of '95: Born to Fail?" (by Preston Townley, Conference Board, at City Club of Chicago)

- "When Will It Be Fun to Fly Again?" (by Robert Aaronson, Air Transport Association, at British-American Business Association)

- "Make a Difference Instead of a Deal" (by David Tappan, Jr., Fluor Corporation, at University of Southern California Graduate School of Business)

- "To Be or Not to Be: The Hamlet Syndrome in Canada" (by R. D. Fullerton, Canadian Imperial Bank of Commerce, at Vancouver Board of Trade)

- "What Would You Do If *Your* Name Were on the Building?" (by Melvin Goodes, Warner-Lambert Company, at Strategic Planning Conference)

  Avoid titles that sound like doctoral dissertations (e.g., "The Inherent Challenges of Economic Redistribution in the 1980s"). Nobody wants to quote anything that sounds like a textbook.

2. *Distribute copies to the audience.* Always do this *after* your presentation, not before. Otherwise, they'll be reading and rustling papers while you're trying to speak.

   One good way: Have assistants at the doors as the audience leaves.

3. *Give a copy to your employee information staff.* Your public relations department may be able to plan a related story for the employee newspaper.

4. *Send an advance copy of the speech to the trade publication that serves your business.* Make the editor's work easier:

- Be sure the speech is easy to read—with short paragraphs and wide margins. (See Chapter 10 for details.) Add subheads to catch the editor's attention.

- Use colored ink to underline a couple of quotable phrases in the speech—phrases the editor can pull out and use in a caption or headline or call-out.

- Attach a one-page summary. This summary may be the only thing the editor bothers to read, so make it good.

- Highlight the speech's main points. Include an impressive statistic or a memorable quote or an interesting example—anything to grab the editor's attention.

5. *Send an advance copy to nearby colleges and universities.*

- The placement office may want to file your speech and share it with students who apply to your company.

- The appropriate department may want to present your ideas in class.

- The campus newspaper may want to cover your speech, especially if its content affects the lives of students.

6. *Prepare news releases for newspapers and local radio/ TV stations.* Make your releases short and snappy. Don't think "corporate." Think "newsworthy/ interesting/important." Put yourself in the shoes of an editor or a news director and ask, "What kind of press release would I like to receive?" The universal answer: "The kind of press release that makes my work easier."
  For newspapers: Give them a good lead, some-

thing they can use "as is." Editors aren't looking for more work. They're looking for good stories to make their work easier. Give them a good lead, and they may give you good coverage.

For radio and TV: Give them three or four short sentences written for the ear and ready to deliver on the air. Remember: News directors receive dozens—often hundreds—of press releases each day. It's human nature for them to use the ones that are "ready to go"—that don't require research and rewriting.

Mail the press releases a few days in advance. Be sure to provide round-the-clock telephone numbers where the editor or news director can contact you.

Note: Some of the smaller radio stations will play excerpts of major speeches. Send them a tape.

7. *Appear on a radio or TV interview program.* The United States has about 800 commercial TV stations and about 8,000 AM and FM radio stations—plus about 5,000 cable stations. Virtually all of them have interview programs where you can appear as a follow-up to your speech. (*Note:* Don't underestimate the smaller, nonprime time shows. They may give you valuable access to certain audiences.)

How can you get booked for an interview program? Call the station about two weeks in advance and let the program director know why the story is newsworthy. Be brief. Program directors have busy schedules and won't listen to a long-winded pitch.

If you sense interest, offer written backup material. Include any recent publications. A book or a magazine feature will increase your credibility. For TV shows, offer to provide visuals—slides, film footage, small-scale models, even documents to lift and show as you make your point.

Television is a highly visual medium. If you offer

to show things to the viewers, you will stand a better chance of getting on the show.

8. *Reprint the speech and take a direct-mail approach.* It is quite inexpensive to issue speech reprints on standard-size business paper with holes punched for easy insertion into loose-leaf binders.

   If your budget allows, you might want to publish a booklet with a bold cover.

   Of course, you don't have to reprint the entire speech. Avon once *condensed* a talk on corporate support for volunteerism and published just these highlights in a glossy brochure entitled "Caring . . . Is Everyone's Business." The brochure used only one 8½ × 11-inch piece of glossy paper, folded into thirds— handy for fitting into a standard #10 business envelope.

   Be sure to consider postage costs when you design your reprints.

9. *Submit a copy to:*

• THE EXECUTIVE SPEAKER
P.O. Box 292437
Dayton, OH 45429
This monthly publication reprints excerpts of speeches on a wide variety of topics. It also serves as a national clearinghouse for business speeches and keeps thousands of noteworthy speeches on file in its library. It's a substantial resource for any businessperson who's interested in becoming a better—and more visible— speaker. Inclusion in this publication can bring your speech to the attention of people in many organizations around the country.

• SPEECHWRITER'S NEWSLETTER
407 South Dearborn
Chicago, IL 60605

This weekly publication runs short, lively excerpts of speeches and cites the names/addresses of their speechwriters.

- VITAL SPEECHES
389 Johnnie Dodd Blvd.
Box 1247
Mount Pleasant, SC 29465
This biweekly publication reprints entire manuscripts of significant speeches. The front cover reads, "The best thought by the best minds on current issues"—and the list of contributors reads like a who's who in international politics and business. This prestigious forum has a tough selection process, but if you've produced a particularly well-written speech on a noteworthy topic, you'll want to make the extra effort to send *Vital Speeches* a copy. I've been able to get considerable attention for my clients through this publication, and I would urge you to consider it as a valuable public relations and marketing tool.

Make the most of your speech. After all, you worked hard to prepare it. Now, make it work hard for *you*.

THIRTEEN

International Speeches

*Az me kumt iber di planken, bakumt men andereh
gedanken.* [If you cross over the fence, you acquire other
ideas.]
—Yiddish proverb

The globalization of business has brought many changes
. . . not the least of which is a critical need to "cross over the
fence" and communicate with international audiences.

An American manufacturer has to give a speech in Eastern Europe . . . Japanese investors must give an important
presentation in California . . . a German banker needs to
address a group of international bankers in London . . . Mexican leaders want to talk about trade agreements with Canadian executives—these are all common assignments in today's
global marketplace.

Unfortunately, few speakers have adequate experience
with international audiences, and they bring many anxieties to
the podium:

- How can I meet the distinctive demands of this foreign
  audience?

- How can I be sure my message is "getting across"?

- How can I use translators effectively?

- How can I avoid the pitfalls of cross-cultural gaffes?

- How can I use humor effectively?

- How can I show respect for my foreign hosts?

- How can I show pride in my own cultural heritage?

The following examples will show how other leaders have dealt with international speaking assignments. Perhaps you can gain some ideas by listening to their techniques.

HOW TO GET YOUR MESSAGE ACROSS IN ANY LANGUAGE

Cite an Expert from Your Host Country

When Dr. Hans Decker, vice chairman of the Siemens Corporation, spoke to the Business Week President's Forum about German education, he cited a noted American educator who had this praise for Germany's educational success:

I'm pleased to say, the German approach to education is starting to gain recognition from educators around the world. Albert Shankar (President of the American Federation of Teachers) visited a school in Cologne and made these observations.

He said, in America, "Eighty-five percent of classroom time is presently taken up by the teacher talking. We work against the team nature of kids."

But, in Germany, Shankar said, "Students are formed into small teams. The same teacher stays with these students for several years. That's continuity, accountability, and community."

Express Your Pleasure at the Privilege of Addressing This Foreign Audience

As the chairman of the Fiat Group, Giovanni Agnelli was asked to give the annual Romanes Lecture at Oxford University in England. He acknowledged the cross-cultural honor this way:

> Over the past hundred years, the Romanes lecture has been given by some of Britain's most illustrious men and women. I believe this is the first time that an Italian has been invited to take the platform at this prestigious event, and I am most grateful to the chancellor and the University of Oxford authorities for according me the honour.
>
> However, I should perhaps warn you that I am an industrialist, *not* an academic, and so I hope you will not expect me to give you a lecture in the strict sense of the word.
>
> What I would like to do instead is to discuss a subject currently of major public interest. . . . *What is Europe?*

Include References to Your Own Cultural Values

When the Emir of Kuwait spoke before a United Nations General Assembly, he opened by giving a short Moslem prayer. And he ended with these moving words:

> The State of Kuwait will remain, as always, faithful to its principles, true to its system of values, close to its friends, and respectful of its obligations and commitments.
>
> Together, we will join hands in concert and harmony to secure our development and progress. This will be a fulfillment of God's promise as rendered in the following verse:
>
> > O ye who believe,
> > If you will aid [the cause of]
> > Allah, He will aid you,

> And plant your feet firmly.
> (Surah 47, *Mohammad, Verse 7)*

And whose word can be truer than Allah's?

Thank you and may Allah, our Lord, bring you all peace and grace.

Use a Quotation That Reflects Your Host Country's Culture

When Herbert Cordt, as member of the managing board at Oesterreichische Laenderbank AG, spoke to the Harvard Club of New York, he ended his speech with an American quotation:

> Ladies and gentlemen: While realizing the risks of a restructuring in Eastern Europe, we also clearly see the huge benefits that will flow from a peaceful Europe that is no longer divided.
> Let me finish with a sentence of an American philosopher-economist who said: "We don't know what the future holds. Therefore, I am an optimist."

Be Vivid

When newly elected Brazilian president Fernando Collor de Mello evaluated the economic situation in his country, he used highly visual details that would make a powerful impression in *any* language:

> I am driving a packed bus at 150 kilometers per hour, headed for a cliff. Either we put on the brakes and some people get a little bruised up, or we go over the edge and we all die.

Stress the Need for Cross-Cultural Communication

Here's how Don Blandin, director of the Business–Higher Education Forum, addressed the issue of cultural diversity in today's global workplace:

> The changing ethnic makeup of America has been felt nowhere more keenly than in our offices and factories. . . .
>
> Today, forty-two percent of new labor force entrants are either immigrants or minorities. That megatrend, which is reshaping both the color and the cultural background of our workforce, presents real challenges on a daily basis to those of you who must manage these workers.
>
> For example, one of Digital Equipment Company's factories in Boston employs three hundred fifty people from forty-four countries, and they speak nineteen languages. Written announcements are printed in Chinese, French, Spanish, Portuguese, Vietnamese, and Haitian Creole—not to mention English. In the new lexicon, America's workplaces are fast becoming "multicultural" and "multiracial."

HOW TO USE A TRANSLATOR

When Joseph Pulitzer published the *World* at the turn of the century, he got the bizarre idea to take his advertising campaign beyond the *earth* and extend it to the entire *universe*. How? By erecting an enormous advertising sign in New Jersey that would be visible on Mars. He abandoned his plan only when an associate asked, "What language would we print it in?"

What language, indeed?

Of course, most translation assignments prove a little more mundane than Mr. Pulitzer's, but ordinary interpretation is demanding nonetheless.

After all, there's a huge difference between someone who happens to speak a foreign language . . . and someone who has the highly developed skills to serve as an interpreter in important business dealings!

The former is an amateur . . . the latter is a professional. Business translation clearly demands a professional . . . and you will get only what you pay for.

If *you* are giving a speech to an audience that speaks another language, how can you find a translator who's adequately skilled for *your* purposes? Try asking these practical questions when interviewing prospective interpreters:

- "Where were you trained?"

- "What are the credentials of your schools/teachers?"

- "What was the nature of your training" (i.e., German literature versus business German)?

- "How often do you work as a translator?" (Yes, foreign language skills *do* get rusty.)

- "Did you ever *live* in this foreign country?"

- "What were your last three translating assignments?" (Ask for specific details: lengths of assignments, types of material, types of clients, unusual circumstances, fees, et cetera. Be sure to request the names of these clients, so you can check for recent references.)

- "Have you ever served as an interpreter within my particular industry?" (This is a critical point. Each business has its own lingo, its own buzz words. You want someone who can translate your distinctive terminology like an "insider.")

In addition, ask *yourself* some questions:

- "Do I feel comfortable with this interpreter?" (Rapport is an important factor! After all, you've got to place a great deal of trust in your translator—and you want to do it with confidence.)

- "Will this person represent me well—in an attractive, well-groomed manner?" (Look at it this way: In the eyes of the audience, your interpreter is literally a stand-in for *you*.)

Here's a final caveat about using a translator—straight from the mouth of President Reagan.

In remarks to the National Governors' Association, President Reagan included this bit of self-deprecating humor about the pitfalls of speaking to a foreign audience:

> As you know, I recently visited Mexico to meet with President de la Madrid. And I was reminded of when I was governor of California and was asked by the then-President to go down and represent him. . . .
>
> On this first visit to Mexico, I gave a speech to a rather large audience and then sat down to rather unenthusiastic and scattered applause. I was embarrassed and tried to cover all of that, because what made it worse was that the next speaker up was speaking in Spanish, which I didn't understand, but he was getting interrupted virtually every line with most enthusiastic applause.
>
> So, I started clapping before anyone else and longer than anyone else until our ambassador learned over and said to me, "I wouldn't do that if I were you. He's interpreting your speech."

THE FINISHING TOUCHES

Consider all of the "little things" you can do to give your international speeches a special flair.

- When H. Norman Schwarzkopf was made an honorary member of the French Foreign Legion at a ceremony near Marseilles, he flattered his audience by delivering his most powerful line in French. Talking to the Foreign Legion officers, he used his best French accent to offer this heartfelt praise: "Your men are great."

- When the cabaret singer Karen Akers was invited to the White House to sing at a state dinner for Polish President Lech Walesa, she got help from the Polish Consulate. After writing her own introductions to her songs in English, she had them translated into Polish . . . and then she received coaching from the consulate staff to help with her pronunciation. As Ms. Akers put it, "I'm just trying to learn enough to demonstrate how happy I am to sing for him."

- When a manager at a U.S. steel company spoke to eager visitors from Eastern Europe, he cared enough to replace all American measures with metric terms.

- When George Bush gave an historic speech in Mainz, Germany, he had it timed for midday delivery . . . perfect for the American TV networks to carry it on their morning news programs back home.

- When Steve Harlan, vice chairman, international, of KPMG Peat Marwick, addressed the benefits of free trade with Mexico, he concluded with an old Mexican proverb. First, he delivered the proverb in its original Spanish *("El que adelante no mirea, atras se queda")*. Then, he paused a moment and offered its English translation: "He who doesn't look ahead, stays behind." By offering the foreign proverb in both languages, he created a more dramatic rapport with his international audience.

FOURTEEN

Speakers Bureaus

It is generally better to deal by speech than by letter.
—Francis Bacon, Lord Chancellor of England

Do these situations sound familiar?

- You're a manager at an electric utility, and customers are worried about the possibility of transmission lines causing cancer. How can you convince the community that your operations are safe?

- You're an administrator at a hospital, you've just expanded your outpatient services, and you'd like more people to know about your new facilities. What's the best way to reach potential patients?

- You're a branch manager at a bank, and you need to pursue new customers more aggressively. How can you persuade people to use the wide spectrum of financial services you offer?

- You're a senior vice president at a telephone company, and you'd like to inform consumers about rapid changes in the telecommunications industry. What's the best way to create community awareness and goodwill?

Consider using a *speakers bureau*. A speakers bureau is an *organized* effort to communicate a company's message to specific target groups—perhaps to the Rotary, or to the Chamber of Commerce, or to women's groups, men's clubs, or school groups.

More and more companies are finding that speakers bureaus are an effective, low-cost way to reach a variety of civic, business, professional, social, and educational organizations . . . in short, to present their corporate message to important constituencies within their community.

Telephone companies, utilities, oil companies, hospitals, nonprofit groups . . . these are just a few of the organizations that have benefited by running effective speakers bureaus.

If you'd like to set up a brand-new speakers bureau for your company . . . or, if you'd like to pump some life into an old bureau that's not very active . . . or, if you'd like to correct some specific problems with an ineffective bureau, read on. These guidelines should help.

MEMBERSHIP

Who can become a member of your speakers bureau? Consider your options:

- Any current employee?

- Either part-time or full-time?

- Both union and management?

- From entry-level to upper management?

- How about the company's retirees? (They typically know the company well, are quite aware of industry issues, have time to donate, enjoy sharing their expertise, and can prove quite credible to audiences.)

SIZE

How large should you make your bureau? Answer: Only as large as you can manage.

After all, what's the sense in having seventy-five members listed with your speakers bureau if you can't book enough speaking engagements to keep them all involved, or if you can't find enough time to supervise each speaker?

A better option: Keep the bureau small, and do a more efficient job of managing each speaker's special talents.

It takes a lot of effort to run a speakers bureau. Too often, top management thinks a speakers bureau can be managed as a part-time chore—dumped on someone in PR, or pushed on to a secretary's desk. That's a misconception.

Consider the risks of:

- booking a date improperly

- choosing the wrong speaker for a particular audience

- having an assigned speaker get sick at the last minute

- forgetting to check audio-visual needs

- providing wrong handouts

- sending out an unprepared, uninteresting speaker

- failing to inform bureau members about changes in company policies

If you don't keep on top of these logistics, you'll discourage your speakers, alienate your audiences, and create alarm among top management. Prevent problems by making sure your bureau has the full-time coordinator it deserves.

TRAINING

Your speakers will be only as good as the training they get. So, decide upfront *how* you wish to train them, and *how often.*

Again, what's the use of having seventy-five members in your bureau if you can't get the budget to train all of them effectively?

Much smarter: Match the size of your membership to your training budget. If you can get only enough money to train forty members each year, then be realistic. Limit the size of your bureau to that number. Better to train forty members well than to train seventy-five members poorly. Don't try to "stretch" your dollars by skipping training sessions—that's no bargain.

PAYMENT/BENEFITS

Will you pay your members for each speech they give? That can be risky.

Wise speakers bureaus generally avoid monetary payment because there are too many variables, too many pitfalls. After all, would it be fair to pay a mediocre speaker the same as a terrific speaker? Would evening or weekend speeches demand higher rates? Would hostile audiences merit larger fees? (And, if so, who's to define a hostile audience?)

Perhaps most important, would a "paid" speaker have as much credibility with an audience as a member who simply volunteers to speak from personal commitment? Remember: Audiences are quick to spot a "hired gun"—and often respond accordingly.

A smarter choice: Offer your speakers *other* forms of compensation. After members have given a significant number of speeches, consider offering some extra vacation time . . . or a complementary make-over session that will improve their podium appearance . . . or the opportunity to take advanced courses in presentation skills . . . or even a simple, heartfelt "thank you" letter (and the knowledge that their efforts will be recognized in upcoming performance reviews).

You'll also need to address the whole issue of expense accounts. Decide *in advance* if you'll reimburse your speakers for taxi fares, car mileage, restaurant meals. And, just as important, decide *in advance* what your limits will be. (Otherwise, you might find yourself paying speakers too much money to dine in fancy restaurants.)

MOTIVATION

Once you've got your members signed up, how can you keep them interested? Consider setting up a simple point system, giving speakers credit for the:

- number of speeches they give
- number of recruits they sign up
- number of new forums they find

With a simple chart, your members can see—at a glance—how their activity level compares with that of other speakers. Put a star by the names of speakers who meet a certain level of productivity.

When Seattle City Light began giving its speakers credit for the number of presentations they gave, the bureau's bookings shot up dramatically—literally quadrupling in the first year! The bureau's coordinator sends quarterly performance reports to all layers of management—creating a higher profile for her speakers and fostering companywide support for the good work of the bureau.

RECOGNITION/REWARDS

Let's face it:

When employees give up a Saturday afternoon to speak at a community event on the company's behalf . . . when they trudge out in a snowstorm to honor a speaking engagement at the Lion's Club . . . when they drop what they're doing to "fill in" as a last-minute speaker at the Rotary . . . well, don't you think they deserve some special recognition?

Here are some ideas:

- Host an annual breakfast/luncheon/dinner for all of the bureau's members. Let your budget determine the meal and the restaurant you choose. Remember: A first-rate breakfast is seen as more luxurious than a third-rate dinner. If you're working with a shoestring budget, skip the restaurant and offer a simple buffet in-house. By using local delis and caterers, you can keep your costs to a minimum.

- Treat your most productive speakers to a special event—perhaps theater tickets, a concert, or a day's pass to a theme park. Allow them to bring along a spouse or friend to make up for all those times when their speaking assignments kept them away from home.

  Each year, the Public Service Electric & Gas Company in New Jersey treats its most active speakers to a festive dinner buffet. The bureau's coordinator invites each speaker to bring along a guest—to show PSE&G's sincere appreciation for all the "private time" these speakers give to the bureau each year.

- Hire a motivational speaker to address the bureau at an annual gathering. This appearance by a professional speaker will not only serve as a reward but also will "rev up" the bureau's members for their own assignments.

Utilities, hospitals, and a wide range of organizations often ask me to speak at their recognition dinners. On these occasions, I make my speeches both informational and motivational—with a good dose of humor. (For example, a typical topic might be: "How to Write & Give a Speech—& Survive!") My goal? To give the bureau members an enjoyable evening—and also inspire them to improve their own speeches.

• Ask the CEO to send your members a personal letter of appreciation. An added touch: Frame the letter, so members can put it on display.

• Send a holiday gift. Include a personal note of appreciation.

The Baptist Medical Centers in Birmingham, Alabama, run a Health Talks speakers bureau that consists of BMC physicians and other health-care professionals. Each December, the coordinator sends a small gift of appreciation (perhaps a potted plant, or a practical desk accessory) to her speakers. To keep costs down, she distributes the token gifts through interoffice mail.

PERFORMANCE STANDARDS

There's no sense in giving speeches unless you know they're accomplishing something. If you provide your audiences with an evaluation form, you'll gain valuable information about the success (or failure) of your bureau's presentations.

Be sure to keep your evaluation forms simple. If you make them complex and time consuming, no one will bother to fill them out—and you'll lose valuable insights into the effectiveness of your speakers bureau.

A simple evaluation form would include these basics:

- Speaker?____excellent____good____fair____poor
- Content?____useful____not relevant to my needs
- What did you like best about the program?____

  _____

- Can you suggest any changes?____

  _____

- What topics would you like to see in the future?____

  _____

- Are you active in any other groups that might like to hear one of our free presentations?____

  _____

  (If so, please give us your name and phone number so we can contact you:)____

  _____

LETTING THE COMMUNITY KNOW ABOUT YOUR PROGRAMS

It doesn't do much good to have terrific speakers in your bureau, if no one knows about them. So, make it a priority to publicize your bureau's programs.

Start by preparing a brochure. It needn't be big or glossy or expensive—just effective. List all the topics covered by your speakers, and provide an interesting capsule summary for each topic. List the members of your speaking team, and cite their credentials. If possible, provide photographs of your speakers—but make sure they're *good* photos (not some blurry, boring head shots you've had lying around the office for the past decade).

Mail the brochure to all the potential groups in your area. (The Chamber of Commerce usually has such a listing.) Call the program chairperson of each group. With luck, you might be able to line up speaking engagements on the spot. At the very least, you can make a friendly contact and follow up another time.

Ask your speakers to help distribute the bureau's brochures—perhaps at their church, or at their monthly Lion's Club meeting, or in their neighborhood, or on the bulletin board at the supermarket, or in their doctor's office. The possibilities are virtually unlimited.

Be sure to send brochures and short press releases to all the local newspapers. The editors may well be able to list your programs in their "community calendar" sections.

APPROPRIATE FORUMS

When you're just starting your speakers bureau, you'll have plenty of available time slots and you'll welcome almost any audience—just to give your speakers something to do!

But, as you receive more speaking invitations, you'll become increasingly choosy about your audiences. After all, you simply won't have enough time to accept every invitation that comes your way.

How to pick and choose the best forums for your purposes? Consider:

- *Size* (Will the audience be large enough to justify your expenditure of time, effort and money?)

- *Type of meeting* (Women's club luncheon? Professional panel meeting? Civic forum? Community event? Senior citizen social gathering? Ask yourself, "Will this meeting give us an *appropriate* forum to deliver our message?")

- *Typical speaker* (Ask: "Who spoke at last month's meeting? And the month before that?" You'll gain some insights into the type of programs they run—and the type of attention/inattention you can expect from this particular audience.)

- *Agenda* (Who else will be speaking/singing/ entertaining/fund-raising/recruiting/et cetera at this event? What other activities will be part of the program? For example, if you've been asked to talk to senior citizens about energy conservation, but the program's *main* event is a bingo game . . . well, read the writing on the wall, decline the invitation, and direct your efforts to an audience where you'll get a more attentive response and a better return on your speaking investment.)

FIFTEEN

Speechwriters: How to Hire One . . . How to work With One

A great speech from the leader to the people eases our
isolation, breaks down the walls, includes people: It takes
them inside a spinning thing and makes them part of the
gravity.
—Peggy Noonan, presidential speechwriter for Ronald
Reagan

When Gerald Ratner, the world's largest jewelry retailer, gave
a speech at London's Albert Hall, he offered these four rules
to becoming a multimillionaire:

1. Understand your market.

2. Form clear quality goals.

3. Evaluate your product against the competition's.

4. Don't write your own speeches.

And, there's some truth in that last point!

The fact is: Very few senior executives have the *time* to
write their own speeches. After all, it's simply not cost effective
for CEOs to spend weeks laboring over a speech when they
should be doing what they're paid to do, which is *run a company*.

What's more, very few senior executives have the *inclination* to write their own speeches. They're business people—not
writers—so it's only natural for them to be more comfortable

managing business details than putting pen to paper (or, finger to keyboard).

And, yes, let's be brutally honest: Very, *very* few senior executives have the *talent* to write their own speeches. After all, speechwriting is a highly demanding specialty . . . so specialized, in fact, that most professional writers can't do it well. Why? Because the process of writing a speech is quite different from writing a memo, or a press release, or a newspaper story—and woe be to anyone who fails to grasp this vital difference.

So, if *you* think you would benefit from hiring the expertise of a professional speechwriter (either on staff or as a freelance/consultant), start by asking other business people for referrals. Then, use these practical questions to help choose someone who's right *for you.*

- "How long have you been writing speeches?"
  You want someone with experience . . . someone who has handled a great number of speechwriting assignments . . . someone who can approach virtually any speaking situation with skill, confidence, and aplomb.

- "Is speechwriting your specialty?"
  This is a critical factor. If the writer is a generalist—that is, someone who does press releases one day, brochures the next, and speeches whenever they come along—you simply won't get the benefit of a well-tuned speechwriter's "ear."
  Tip: The location of your business need not limit you. Even if you operate out of a small town, you still have access to top speechwriting talent. A phone and a FAX machine will connect you with speechwriters all over the country. So, don't limit yourself unnecessarily by imposing geographical restrictions.

- "Do you do all of the speechwriting yourself—or, do you subcontract some assignments?"

I cannot stress this point enough. Beware of any firm that takes a "group approach" to speechwriting.

Case in point: Many public relations firms will try to impress the client by sending high-ranking representatives to preliminary meetings, but then secretly "farm out" the actual speechwriting job to an unidentified freelancer. Quite often, to cut corners, PR firms choose the least-expensive freelancers they can get—and then the client (who paid top dollar to get a big-name PR firm) wonders why the submitted speech looks so amateurish.

One other serious consideration: If a PR firm subcontracts its speeches to freelance writers you don't know, how can you be sure your material is being treated confidentially? How can you be sure the unseen/unscreened freelancers aren't also taking assignments from your competitors?

Again, you're always better off developing a one-on-one relationship with a professional speechwriter you can trust implicitly.

- "Who are your current/recent clients?"

- "Do you have long-standing relationships with your clients? For example, how many speeches have you done for the XYZ Corporation?"

- "What do you know about the issues my industry faces?"

  Professional speechwriters prepare for interviews by reading about your company and your industry. Accept nothing less.

- "What's your educational background?"

  Caution: Don't think speechwriters need a particular degree in communications, public relations, or journalism. That's a misconception.

  What matters is a bright mind, a keen understanding of the world, a knack for creative listening, an ability to learn new material quickly, a sensitivity about language, and a deep love for the spoken word.

- "What's your professional background?"

   Another caution: Nobody really *begins* a career as a speechwriter. No twenty-two-year-old, fresh out of college and lacking real-life business experience, steps into a speechwriting slot and simply keeps moving up the speechwriting ladder, decade after decade. (And if they did . . . well, frankly, I'd be highly suspicious of their too-narrow background!) Speechwriting is often the culmination of several dynamic career interests.

- "Can you offer constructive criticism?"

   No head-nodders who will say anything to please the boss! You're looking for a bright individual who can tell you what you're doing wrong with your speeches—and show you how to improve.

- "Can you work quickly?"

   Here's an all-too-common scenario:

   Over two months ago, you asked your PR department to write an important speech, but they got tied up producing the annual report or fielding media questions or dealing with an employee crisis . . . whatever.

   Anyhow, they waited until the last minute to write your speech, and now (not surprisingly!) their draft looks like it was slapped together during a lunch hour.

   You're dissatisfied. You're frustrated. You wanted a *terrific* speech for this important occasion, and now you're stuck with only five days left.

   It's times like these when you're glad you've already got a freelance speechwriter listed in your address book—someone you can depend on to work quickly and produce a quality manuscript. Treat this person like gold.

   If you *don't* already know a speechwriter like this,

resolve to start interviewing *now* so you'll never be caught unprepared again.

• "Would you provide recommendations from your clients?"

Be specific. Ask for names and titles. For example, a beginning speechwriter might brag that he's worked for "many executives at Fortune 50 companies"—when, in fact, he did only one actual assignment involving a group of mid-level managers. Learn to probe for references and honest responses.

• "Would you show me some samples of your work?"

Warning: Truly professional speechwriters do *not* pass out samples casually. They're discreet. They consider their speeches to be the property of their clients. So, respect their professionalism and don't ask to see any confidential material.

A much better alternative: Speechwriters can provide *excerpts* of recent speeches, or they can individually ask their clients for permission to distribute a particular manuscript.

• "Do your speeches get media coverage?"

Top speechwriters know how to write attention-getting speeches that prove irresistibly quotable to reporters. Their speeches are often reprinted in *Vital Speeches,* or quoted in the *New York Times,* or cited in significant trade publications.

These speechwriters can help you get valuable media attention for your company—attention that will enhance your professional status, promote your products, tout your services, build credibility for your organization, and draw attention to the issues of your industry.

Not surprisingly, these speechwriters can command more money. They are well worth it.

• "Would you be willing to look at three of my recent speeches and offer a critique?"

Naturally, since you're asking a professional writer to do professional work, you need to offer payment. Only a nonprofessional would accept an assignment without pay.

• "Would you accept a short speechwriting assignment so I can see the way we'd work together?"

It doesn't have to be a big speech, the first time around. Just assign something short—say, an introduction, or a retirement tribute, or an award presentation, something that will allow the two of you to work together as a team on an exploratory basis.

Again, you will need to pay for this initial assignment—perhaps not top dollar, but certainly a respectable fee.

• "Would you describe your fee structure?"

You have a right to ask for cost estimates in advance. Your speechwriter may well offer you a price *range,* depending on how complex the assignment becomes. For example, if a speech requires two on-site meetings, it will cost more than if the same speech could be accomplished via phone and FAX.

Remember: To your speechwriter, time *is* money. The more efficient and streamlined the process, the lower the total fee.

Consider also the deadline you're giving the speechwriter. The tighter the deadline, the greater the fee.

Experienced speechwriters are used to being brought in at the last minute, and they're used to working nights, weekends, and holidays to help clients beat a deadline. But, be aware: They *will* charge more for these rush assignments.

So, if you ask professional speechwriters to do some rush assignments over Thanksgiving weekend,

they may well give up their holiday plans to accommodate you . . . but they'll charge accordingly.

And, come to think of it, you wouldn't have it any
other way, would you?

APPENDIX
Useful Reference Books from the Author's Personal Library

AGE/BIRTHDAY BOOKS

Morris, Desmond. *The Book of Ages.* New York: Penguin, 1983, $8.95. Suppose you want to say a few words at someone's sixtieth birthday party. Turn to this book and find out "who did what" at age sixty. You'll find all sorts of anecdotes, trivia, and quotations for each year of life:

- *Age fifty-two:* Lady Astor quipped, "I refuse to admit that I'm more than fifty-two, even if that does make my sons illegitimate."

- *Age seventy-two:* Maurice Chevalier announced, "Old age isn't so bad when you consider the alternative."

Sampson, Anthony and Sally. *The Oxford Book of Ages.* New York: Oxford University Press, 1988, $7.95. A real kaleidoscope of opinions about every age of life:

- *Age twenty-nine:* "When you come to my epitaph, Charles, let it be in these delicious words, 'She had a long twenty-nine.' " (Rosalind, in James Barrie's *Rosalind*)

- *Age fifty:* "The years between fifty and seventy are the hardest. You are always being asked to do things, and yet you are not decrepit enough to turn them down." (T. S. Eliot)

- *Age seventy-five:* "I am ready to meet my Maker. Whether my Maker is prepared for the ordeal of meeting me is another matter." (Winston Churchill)

ANECDOTES

Fadiman, Clifton. *The Little, Brown Book of Anecdotes.* New York: Little, Brown, 1985, $29.95. An invaluable collection. More than 4,000 well-researched anecdotes about 2,000 famous people—from Hank Aaron to J. P. Morgan to Dylan Thomas. Offers an index of subjects, an index of names, a source list, and a bibliography. (Great for browsing, too!)

Van Ekeren, Glenn. *The Speaker's Sourcebook.* Englewood Cliffs, New Jersey: Prentice-Hall, 1988, $14.95. A wide range of anecdotes and quotations—many of them inspirational and motivational. You'll find Casey Stengel on Leadership . . . Ted Turner on Self-Confidence . . . Woodrow Wilson on Goals. No index, no source list.

BUSINESS

Eigen, Lewis and Siegel, Jonathan. *The Manager's Book of Quotations.* New York: AMACOM, 1989, $24.95. Well-researched quotations covering 47 topics that concern managers:

- *Public Relations:* "We're not paying you to make us look like a bunch of idiots. We're paying you so others won't find out we're a bunch of idiots." (anonymous executive to PR firm president)

- *Motivation:* "Genius is initiative on fire." (Holbrook Jackson)

- *Corporate Culture:* "Excellent firms don't believe in excellence—only in constant improvement and constant change." (Tom Peters)

Griffith, Joe. *Speaker's Library of Business Stories, Anecdotes, and Humor.* Englewood Cliffs, New Jersey: Prentice-Hall, 1990, $14.95. An outstanding collection of fresh material covering two hundred business topics:

- *Future:* "We know only two things about the future: It cannot be known, and it will be different from what exists now and from what we now expect." (Peter Drucker)

- *Optimism:* Learn about the test that Metropolitan Life developed to sort the optimists from the pessimists when hiring sales personnel.

- *Promotions:* "Every time your superiors promote you, they are in effect saying to your peers and subordinates: 'This person possesses the qualities we'd like to see in more of our workers.' " (Donald Seibert, CEO, J. C. Penney)

- *Time Management:* Learn about Ben Franklin's method for dealing with time-wasters (a great story to use with groups of sales people).

Hay, Peter. *The Book of Business Anecdotes.* New York: Facts on File, 1988, $22.95. Conveniently organized by subject—from Money, to Selling, to Corporate Culture. Includes good stories about Alexander Graham Bell's telephone system . . . John Wanamaker's mastery of advertising . . . T. S. Eliot's short-lived experience as a bank clerk . . . and more.

CALENDAR/DAILY LISTINGS

Spinrad, Leonard and Thelma. *Complete Speaker's Almanac.* Englewood Cliffs, New Jersey: Prentice-Hall, 1984, $14.95. Suppose you must give a speech on June 2. Pick up this book, and you'll find several entries listing things that happened on this date in history. For example, June 2, 1943, saw the Battle of the Warsaw Ghetto. June 2, 1787, saw Ben Franklin speak at the Constitutional Convention, arguing that no salaries should be paid to the executive branch (most especially, the President).

DEFINITIONS

Brussell, Eugene E. *Webster's New World Dictionary of Quotable Definitions.* Englewood Cliffs, New Jersey: Prentice-Hall, 1988, $29.95. Want a clever definition? Forget your regular dictionary. Turn to this book for more than 17,000 memorable definitions and zippy one-liners on 2,000 subjects, including:

- *Ambassador:* "A paid political tourist." (anonymous)

- *Lecturer:* "Traveling men who express themselves and collect." (Shannon Fife)

- *Public Opinion:* "What people think that other people think." (Alfred Austin)

Evans, Ivor H. *Brewer's Dictionary of Phrase and Fable.* New York: Harper & Row, 1981, $24.95. A gold mine of wonderful information about popular phrases, fables, history, religion, archeology, the arts, and sciences. Especially useful when you're trying to create clever titles for your speeches.

DIRECTORIES

The Monitor Publishing Company offers directories dealing with government, corporate, and professional leaders. These directories can give you access (by mail, telephone, or FAX) to top-ranked world executives, to national policymakers, and to state administrators. For a descriptive catalog of titles, contact: Monitor Publishing Company, 104 Fifth Avenue, 2nd Floor, New York, NY, 10011, telephone (212) 627-4140.

EDUCATION

Bronner, Simon J. *Piled Higher and Deeper: The Folklore of Campus Life.* Little Rock, Arkansas: August House Publishers, 1990, $9.95. Well-researched folklore dealing with such campus realities as final exams, absentminded professors, homecoming, jocks, faculty, fraternity pledging, and graduation.

ETHNIC

Weinreich, Beatrice Silverman. *Yiddish Folktales.* New York: Pantheon Books, 1988, $21.95. Nearly 200 marvelous tales (never before published) from the vivid world of East European Jewry. These stories are all rich in custom, history, wit, and imagination. *Special Note:* The Pantheon Fairy Tale and Folklore Library also publishes enchanting collections of folklore from Africa, Japan, Ireland, to name a few places.

West, John O. *Mexican-American Folklore.* Little Rock, Arkansas: August House Publishers, 1988, $9.95. Legends, songs, proverbs, tales of saints, stories of revolutionaries, and much more. *Special Note:* August House prides itself on an outstanding American Folklore Series, representing about a dozen cultures. For information about other titles, send a self-addressed stamped envelope to August House Publishers, Inc., P.O. Box 3223, Little Rock, Arkansas, 72203.

HUMOR

Braude, Jacob M. *Braude's Treasury of Wit and Humor.* Englewood Cliffs, New Jersey: Prentice-Hall, 1964, $9.95. Lighthearted material, arranged alphabetically by topic. For example, under "Real Estate" you'll find:

"There are advantages and disadvantages about this property," said the honest real estate agent.

"To the north is the gas works, to the east a glue factory, to the south a fish and chip shop, and to the west a sewage farm. Those are the disadvantages."

"What are the advantages?" asked the buyer.

"You can always tell which way the wind is blowing," said the agent.

Jones, Loyal and Billy Edd Wheeler. *Hometown Humor, U.S.A.* Little Rock, Arkansas: August House Publishers, 1991, $19.95. Homespun humor from regular folks, as well as celebrities like Minnie Pearl and Senator Sam Ervin. Topics include: Aging, Health, Farmers, Education, Law, Politics, Preachers, and City Folks.

Metcalf, Fred. *The Penguin Dictionary of Modern Humorous Quotations.* London: Penguin, 1986, $10.95. Useful for speakers and writers, and fun for browsers. Offers a decidedly British bent. Alphabetical by topic:

- *Conferences:* "A conference is a gathering of important people who singly can do nothing, but together can decide that nothing can be done." (Fred Allen)

- *Neville Chamberlain:* "Listening to a speech by Chamberlain is like paying a visit to Woolworth's. Everything in its place and nothing above sixpence." (Aneurin Bevan, speech, House of Commons, 1937)

- *Television:* "Time has convinced me of one thing. Television is for appearing on, not looking at." (Noel Coward)

- *Wealth:* "The rich are the scum of the earth in every country." (G. K. Chesterton)

Perret, Gene and Linda. *Funny Business.* Englewood Cliffs, New Jersey: Prentice-Hall, 1990, $12.95. Chock-full of funny one-liners on virtually every aspect of business:

- *Personnel:* " 'Personnel' is now 'Human Resources.' It's the only department in all of industry that operates under an alias."

- *Mandatory Retirement:* "The company doesn't want you when you're old and useless. They prefer people who are young and useless."

- *Resumes:* "Resumes are hard to read. It's the combination of white lies on white paper."

MILITARY

Charlton, James. *The Military Quotation Book.* New York: St. Martin's Press, 1990, $12.95. Lots of fine quotes:

- "All wars are popular for the first thirty days." (Arthur Schlesinger, Jr.)

- "If I had learned to type, I never would have made brigadier general." (Brigadier General Elizabeth P. Hoisington)

- "A hero is no braver than an ordinary man, but he is brave five minutes longer." (Ralph Waldo Emerson)

Unfortunately, no chapters or subject index, so it takes a while to find what you want.

Hastings, Max. *The Oxford Book of Military Anecdotes.* New York: Oxford University Press, 1986, $7.95. An impressively researched anthology, arranged chronologically. Includes an index of principal names and places, but no subject listing or chapter heads (which can be frustrating if you're trying to find something in a hurry).

POLITICAL STORIES AND QUOTATIONS

Henning, Charles. *The Wit & Wisdom of Politics.* Golden, Colorado: Fulcrum, 1989, $12.95. Good cross-section of sources:

- *Mario Cuomo:* "You campaign in poetry, you govern in prose."

- *Jerry Brown:* "Too often I find that the volume of paper expands to fill the available briefcase."

- *Golda Meir:* "Whether women are better than men I cannot say— but they are certainly no worse."

PROVERBS

Auden, W. H. and Kronenberger, Louis. *The Viking Book of Aphorisms.* New York: Penguin Books, 1966, $6.95. Where else would you find this gem by Goethe: "Know thyself? If I knew myself, I'd run away." More than 3,000 wise and pithy comments.

Fergusson, Rosalind. *The Penguin Dictionary of Proverbs.* New York: Penguin Books, 1983, $5.95. Handy proverbs arranged in easy-to-use chapters.

PUBLICITY

Caruba, Alan. *Power Media Selects: The Nation's Most Influential Media Elite.* Washington, D.C.: Broadcast Interview Source, 1992, $166.50. A selective listing of media "influentials," that is, editors, journalists, and producers who can help you target your message either to the largest number or to the most specific segment of the American audience.

Gebbie, Amalia. *Gebbie Press All-in-One Directory.* New Paltz, New York: 1992, $85. Offers wide scope of media contacts: daily newspapers, weekly newspapers, AM-FM radio stations, television stations, general (consumer) magazines, business papers, trade press, Black-Hispanic press, farm publications, news syndicates. All in a single, well-organized, easy-to-use volume.

New York Publicity Outlets. New Milford, Connecticut: Public Relations Plus, 1992, $130. A detailed, neatly organized volume devoted strictly to publicity outlets in metropolitan New York City (that is, within a fifty-mile radius of Columbus Circle). *Note:* This publisher also offers a similar volume devoted to media opportunities in California.

RESEARCH

Berkman, Robert I. *Find It Fast.* New York: Harper & Row, 1987, $6.95. Shows how to discover hidden information sources, how to locate top experts, how to use government data.

Horowitz, Lois. *Knowing Where to Look: The Ultimate Guide to Research.* Cincinnati, Ohio: Writer's Digest Books, 1984, $15.95. How to use everything from libraries to embassies to newspapers to videotext systems. Helps you avoid time-consuming research traps, frustrating dead-ends, and common pitfalls.

QUOTATIONS (GENERAL)

Bartlett, John. *Bartlett's Familiar Quotations.* Boston: Little, Brown, 1980, $22.95. A standard reference work, with more than 22,000 quotations. Especially strong in the Bible, the classics, and Shakespeare. Newly revised and updated to include more contemporary figures—such as Muhammad Ali and Mick Jagger. Outstanding index.

Camp, Wesley D. *What a Piece of Work Is Man!* Englewood Cliffs, New Jersey: Prentice-Hall, 1990, $12.95. An outstanding collection of unfamiliar quotations covering 4,000 years of human experience. Well organized, well documented. Alphabetical topics include:

- *Health:* "If you wish to keep as well as possible, the less you think about your health the better." (Oliver Wendell Holmes)

- *Neuroses:* "A neurotic is the person who builds a castle in the air; a psychotic is the person who lives in it; and a psychiatrist is the person who collects the rent." (anonymous)

- *Women's Movement:* "Whatever women do, they must do twice as well as men to be thought half as good. Luckily, this is not difficult." (Charlotte Whitton, former mayor of Ottawa)

Frost, Elizabeth. *The Bully Pulpit.* New York: Facts on File, 1988, $23.95. The cream of presidential quotes covering dozens of subject areas: budgets, work, states rights, negotiations, defense, elections.

Marsden, C. R. S. *Dictionary of Outrageous Quotations.* Topsfield, Massachusetts: Salem House, 1988, $9.95. Feeling cantankerous? Want to nudge your audience with a flip comment? You'll probably find it in here.

Mencken, H. L. *A New Dictionary of Quotations.* New York: Knopf, 1987, $40. A magnificent volume. Superbly researched and annotated. What's more, you can find things easily! Notable for providing the thoughts of significant historical figures (including Karl Marx, John Locke, and the Popes). Many of these quotations simply aren't available in other collections.

Simpson, James B. and Boorstin, Daniel J. *Simpson's Contemporary Quotations.* Boston: Houghton Mifflin, 1988, $19.95. This is not the place to find out what Wordsworth said about daffodils, but if you're looking for post-1950 quotes, you'll find 10,000 of them here. Plus, you'll find separate chapters for each profession (armed forces, medicine, architecture, the press, et cetera). Easy to use. Includes a helpful table of contents, an index of sources, and an index of subjects and key lines.

RELIGION/PHILOSOPHY

Peale, Dr. Norman Vincent. *My Favorite Quotations.* New York: Giniger, 1990, $12.95. Here, the best-selling author of *The Power of Positive Thinking* shares his favorite quotes on a variety of subjects: daily life, enthusiasm, God's creation, relationships, mental health, pain and suffering, healing, community, aging.

Telushkin, Joseph. *Uncommon Sense.* New York: Shapolsky Publishers, 1987, $14.95. From Maimonides to Freud—with seldom-seen contributions by notable rabbis.

- *Haffetz Hayyim* (Polish rabbi): "In the final analysis, for the believer there are no questions, and for the non-believer there are no answers."

- *Woody Allen:* "It seems the world was divided into good and bad people. The good ones slept better . . . while the bad ones seemed to enjoy the waking hours much more."

The book is divided into sections based on the traditional categories of the Jewish commandments. Good historical details, but no index.

Tomlinson, Gerald. *Treasury of Religious Quotations.* Englewood Cliffs, New Jersey: Prentice-Hall, 1991, $14.95. Organized into 149 topics (from Achievement and Duty, to Sorrow and Values), and subdivided into 30 religions and beliefs. For example, the category Forgiveness includes:

- *Christianity:* "Pardon one another so that later on you will not remember the injury. The recollection of an injury is . . . a rusty arrow and poison for the soul." (St. Francis of Paola)

- *Islam:* "He who forgives, and is reconciled unto his enemy, shall receive his reward from Allah." (Koran)

- *Judaism:* "It is fitting for a great God to forgive great sinners." (Talmud)

Well, Albert M., Jr. *Inspiring Quotations.* Nashville: Thomas Nelson, 1988, $11.95. More than 3,000 quotes from leading evangelicals, poets, philosophers, et cetera. Chapters range from Abortion and Atheism to World Peace and Worship—with strong emphasis on fundamental Christian concerns.

- *God's Will:* "God's will is not an itinerary, but an attitude." (Andrew Dhuse)

- *Pride:* "God sends no one away empty except those who are full of themselves." (Dwight L. Moody)

- *Surrender:* "The altar is not a bargain counter where you haggle with God. With Him it is all or nothing." (Lance Zavitz)

Winokur, Jon. *Zen to Go.* New York: New American Library, 1989, $14.95. Bite-sized bits of wisdom from a real cross-section of thinkers—from the Buddha to Jack Kerouac, from Lao Tzu to Kurt Vonnegut.

- *Alan Watts:* "Trying to define yourself is like trying to bite your own teeth."

- *Aldous Huxley:* "There's only one corner of the universe you can be certain of improving, and that's your own self."

- *John Berry:* "The bird of paradise alights only upon the hand that does not grasp."

- *J. Robert Oppenheimer:* "There are children playing in the street who could solve some of my top problems in physics, because they have modes of sensory perception that I lost long ago."

Includes a selected bibliography, but no index.

SPORTS

Tomlinson, Gerald, ed. *Speaker's Treasury of Sports Anecdotes, Stories, & Humor.* Englewood Cliffs, New Jersey: Prentice-Hall, 1990, $12.95. Entries cover 54 different sports and activities, including:

- *Football:* From coach Duffy Daugherty: "When you're playing for the national championship, it's not a matter of life or death. It's more important than that."

- *Skiing:* When Jean-Claude Killy was asked about his education as an Olympic skier, he said, "I learned that you cannot be taught anything by anyone but yourself."

- *Soccer:* Dartmouth coach Whitey Burnham's advice to players: "Be like ducks—calm on the surface and paddling like hell underneath."

- *Baseball:* Casey Stengel's ability to judge potential: "See that fella over there? He's 20 years old. In 10 years, he's got a chance to be a star. Now, that fella over there, he's 20 years old. In 10 years, he's got a chance to be 30."

- *Horse racing:* Elbert Hubbard once quipped, "The only man who makes money following the races is the one who does so with a broom and a shovel."

STATISTICS

The World Almanac and Book of Facts. New York: Pharos Books, Annual, $6.95. An outstanding reference value. Filled with facts about geography, politics, historical events, the arts, and much more. Excellent index, with both general subject headings and specific names.

TOASTS/ROASTS/TRIBUTES

Detz, Joan. *Can You Say a Few Words?* New York: St. Martin's Press, 1991, $10.95. Designed for special occasions. Shows how to prepare and deliver award presentations, retirement tributes, acceptance speeches, eulogies, building dedications, prayers, sports banquets, honorary degrees, anniversary tributes, wedding and birthday toasts, patriotic ceremonies, and more. Also shows how to conquer nervousness, and how to add sparkle to your speeches so they're as memorable as the occasions themselves.

McManus, Ed and Nicholas, Bill. *We're Roasting Harry Tuesday Night.* Englewood Cliffs, New Jersey: Prentice-Hall, 1988, $17.95. How to plan, write, and conduct the business/social roast. Includes ready-to-use lines:

- "He does the work of two men: Laurel and Hardy."

- "Harry's a 'One-Minute Manager.' That's not his philosophy or anything; that's just how long he can carry it off."

- "For the first thirty years of our lives, Harry and I never exchanged an unkind word. Then, we met."

Pasta, Elmer. *Complete Book of Roasts, Boasts and Toasts.* West Nyack, New York: Parker Publishing, 1982, $19.95. Suppose you need to say a few words about an attorney. This book will give you:

- *Roasts:* "She doesn't encourage her clients to commit perjury in court. She does it for them."

- *Boasts:* "I'm such a great lawyer. Once I got the jury so confused they sent the judge to jail."

- *Toasts:* "Let's lift a toast to a great lawyer. He knows it's often better to know the judge than to know the law."

WOMEN

Partnow, Elaine. *The Quotable Woman* (I & II). New York: Facts on File, 1985, $14.95 per volume. This is the first collection of quotations by women. Volume I covers Eve to 1799; volume II covers 1800–1981. Most speakers will find the second volume more practical for their work. Detailed subject index. Helpful biographical index.

Additional copies of *How To Write & Give a Speech* and its companion volume, *Can You Say a Few Words?* (see description below) may be purchased from most booksellers or by mail with the order form on the opposite page. Substantial discounts on orders of 10 or more copies of each book are available for groups and corporate accounts. For more information, call:

St. Martin's Press
Special Sales Department
Toll-free (800) 221-7945, extension # 645
In New York State (212) 674-5151, extension # 645

"Let me say a few words about Joan Detz: Her books are great."
—Roger Ailes, top presidential and corporate communications consultant, and author of *You Are the Message*

"Can You Say a Few Words? by Joan Detz has helped me to speak better. I recommend this book to anyone who wishes to use words well."
—Norman Vincent Peale

Ordering Information

All orders must be prepaid . . . sorry, no CODs.
Please include the following for postage and handling:

Book orders $9.01 - $15.00	include $2.50
Book orders $10.01 - $30.00	include $3.00
Book Orders $30.01 - $40.00	include $4.00
Book orders $40.01 - $50.00	include $4.50
Book orders $50.01-$75.00	include $5.00

Book orders $75.01 and over, add additional $1.00 for each additional $25.00 of order.

Payment must be in U.S. funds, drawn on a U.S. bank.
Canadian Postal Money Orders in U.S. funds accepted.

VISA, Mastercharge, and American Express accepted. $10.00 minimum order not including postage.
Orders over $10.00 may be called in by using our 800 telephone service: 1-800-288-2131.

....

VISA/Mastercharge/
American Express Card Number_____

Expiration Date_____ Signature_____

Quantity	Book Title	Unit Price	Total
	How To Write & Give a Speech	$00.00	
	Can You Say a Few Words?	$10.95	
		Total	
		Sales Tax (NY res.)	
		Sales Tax (NY res.)	
		Shipping/handling	

Ship to:_____

Name:_____

City_____ State_____

Zip_____

Index